A Fascinating Journey to Success
A Professor and CEO True Story

The Island Heaven

First Edition

Richard T. Cheng

Copyright © 2020 by Richard T. Cheng.

ISBN 978-1-952835-23-0 (softcover)
ISBN 978-1-952835-24-7 (ebook)

All rights reserved. No part of this book may be reproduced or transmitted in any form or by any means, electronic or mechanical, including photocopying, recording, or by any information storage and retrieval system without express written permission from the author, except in the case of brief quotations embodied in critical reviews and certain other non-commercial uses permitted by copyright law.

Printed in the United States of America.

Book Vine Press
2516 Highland Dr.
Palatine, IL 60067

CONTENTS

Foreword 5

Chapter 1	My Paradise 7
Chapter 2	Explosion in the Harbor 15
Chapter 3	Ventures in the Paradise 24
Chapter 4	The Turning Point 43
Chapter 5	Good-bye, Lion 57
Chapter 6	The Road to Adulthood 62
Chapter 7	Drowning After a Typhoon 78
Chapter 8	Critical Decisions 91
Chapter 9	A Genius 107
Chapter 10	Rioting against the Americans 112
Chapter 11	The Young Entrepreneurs 118
Chapter 12	The Military Service 133
Chapter 13	My New Experience of Life 138
Chapter 14	The Big Medal 156
Chapter 15	In Love and Marriage 163
Chapter 16	Leaving Taiwan 181

Chapter 17 Typhoon and the Seasick Shepherd 188
Chapter 18 Lost on the High Seas 197
Chapter 19 Handy Man on Board 200
Chapter 20 Arriving in My Dreamland.......................................206

FOREWORD

He was called the $240 Million Professor by the *Transpacific Magazine* on its May 1994 issue. As a result, he was bestowed the honor of many awards, including that given by President Bush in the White House in September 1991.

This book *A Professor and CEO True Story* truthfully described events that happened in his life. It included so much ventures and so many characters. Sometimes it was very moving, and other times it was funny. It is indeed very interesting to read the whole book to find out how a country boy could be so successful to become the $240 Million Professor.

The second volume *The Island Heaven* described the peaceful life he first enjoyed in Taiwan. He was involved in a mishap that almost killed him when experimenting with gunpowder. He was almost drowned in the ocean when he went for swimming after a typhoon. In the military training camp, he wrote three proposals for electronic-controlled weapons. That proposal was accepted by the Defense Department and implemented. As a result, he was awarded a medal. Then he fell in love and got married. He realized the USA was the mecca for technology, so he decided to go to the USA. Because of lack of fund, he decided to take a cargo ship. The ship was hit by a large typhoon and had lost it bearings. Finally, after thirty-three days, he arrived at his destination.

CHAPTER 1

MY PARADISE

I spotted Baba standing next to his Jeep and ran toward him as Mama walked slowly behind. The ground now felt warbling under her feet after staying on the ship for more than a day. Lion ran with me for the fifty-foot dash. When he got close to Baba, he was jumping, whining, and swinging his bushy tail back and forth rapidly. Baba looked happy as he put his hands on my shoulders.

"I am so glad you and Mama came out safely," Baba told me as he bent down to pet Lion. "I don't believe Lion has come all the way with us from Nanjing and is still in such good shape."

"Baba, he has been behaving well on the road, all the way here," I said.

Mama finally caught up with us. Baba assisted her to climb up the Jeep for our new home. She was still dizzy but tried to put on a warm smile. I lifted Lion and put him inside the Jeep.

"Baba, do you like Taiwan so far?" I asked as we were climbing into the Jeep.

"I have been here just three days, but I already like it. Taiwan's condition is much better than what people said about it when we were in Fu-chow," Baba told me.

"Can we buy food conveniently here?" Mama asked.

"I have not seen the market here, but people have told me everything here is better than they had expected. You can find it out yourself soon," Baba said.

"Baba, where are we going?" I could not wait to find out and asked while the Jeep was rolling.

"We are going to a new house the Shore Command just built for us. It is in Si-Tze Bay, a very pretty place. You will see it very soon," Baba said with a smile.

Along the streets we drove through, I found Taiwan very much different from what I had anticipated. The streets were clean, the commercial buildings were mostly two or three stories tall, and many of the residential houses were Japanese style and walled in. People dressed much the same as on the mainland, but I saw many people wearing wooden slippers on the street. Along the way, I was attracted by numerous electronics and mechanical vendors selling parts and surplus equipment. They looked like those left over by the Japanese and American military establishments. I almost asked Baba to let me off right there to take a quick look at the interesting "junk," as Mama called them. I knew then that I would have a lot fun in Taiwan.

We rode in the Jeep for about twenty-five minutes from the pier to a big tunnel entrance. After they saw Baba and recognized him, the heavily armed guards let us pass and we entered this large, long, and dark tunnel.

"We are in the tunnel under the Sou Mountain. This is a restricted military area. No civilians can enter the tunnel," Baba told us.

"Can I come and go through this tunnel when I want to?" I was afraid I might not be able to go to the city freely.

"Sure, you can go out and come back in through the guards. They will know you live inside the compound," Baba assured me.

Once in the tunnel, my eyes were not adjusted fast enough to see what it was like inside. It took me at least one minute to be able to see the old concrete inner walls, full of brownish mildew patches and a few leaky cracks at the far end of the tunnel. After about five or six minutes of slow driving in the tunnel, we exited into an unbelievably beautiful and dreamy world of tall palm trees, giant banyan trees, exotic flowers, white sand beach, clear blue water, and the purest deep-blue sky.

"What a beautiful place!" Mama exclaimed. "I have never seen anywhere so pretty in my life. Look at that big flower tree! Don't they look like many small red lanterns hanging on the tree?"

"I knew you will like this place," Baba said with a smile. He was very happy too.

I understood then why people called this location the "Si-Tze Bay." According to Chinese folklore, Si-Tze was the most beautiful girl in Chinese history. Inside the tunnel, I estimated the land area at two miles by five hundred yards along the coast of South China Sea. Baba told us the Shore Defense Command had just built a residential compound for its married senior officers. Eight duplexes were assigned to the sixteen families. The commanding general and his family occupied a stand-alone ranch house next to the duplexes.

The native Taiwanese and mainland people who had recently moved to Taiwan called Taiwan the Treasure Island. I was sure they meant the island itself was a treasure for people and not because there are treasures to be discovered on this island. Ancestors of Taiwanese mainly came from Fujian Province and had lived here for many generations. The Taiwanese dialect is identical to that of southern Fujian, such as Xia-man and other southern Fujian coastal cities. The island was occupied by the Japanese for fifty years and was repatriated to China in 1946 after the end of World War II. Prior to the Japanese, the Dutch government had occupied Taiwan for more than a century and they named Taiwan Formosa. Because of the long history, most of the westerners knew this island as Formosa but not its real name of Taiwan.

The Si-Tze Bay was a restricted area under military control when the Japanese high command had taken residence in one of the big buildings on the beach. Now the Republic of China—ROC—had placed the area under the control of the Shore Defense

Command. Armed guards were posted at the tunnel entrance and on the road along the shore. Two more guard posts were placed on the west side of the mountain. The area was completely isolated to the outside civilian world. For us, the tunnel was the short and quick link to the city. It was about three quarters of a mile long, straight, and wide enough to allow two-way truck traffic. It was a concrete semicircle with each side of the tunnel wall at six feet high. A few hanging light bulbs were distributed sparsely throughout the length of the tunnel. The lights were so dim that sunlight from the two ends, during the day, provided more visibility in the tunnel than the dim light bulbs.

We were assigned a three-bedroom duplex that was the largest house, besides our own house in Fu-chow, we had lived alone since the war against Japan. In addition to the three bedrooms, it had a large living room, a den, a full bath, and a kitchen. All residents in the compound were high-ranking commanders of the Shore Defense Command. Baba was a colonel who served as the Head of Staff in the command. Our house was one of the larger units in the compound. Baba, Mama, and I shared the house with Lion. After we walked into the house, the first place Mama went to check out was the kitchen. She turned the water on and off in the washbasin and checked the stove, and she was surprised to see all cooking equipment was completely furnished.

"The command is so nice. They thought about everything," Mama beamed. "You know when we left Fu-chow in a hurry we didn't bring anything from the house except Lion and a handbag."

"I sure know that is the case, so I asked Mrs. Shao next door help me to buy the pieces for us. The place was totally empty when it was turned to me couple days ago," said Baba. "I also had some help from other friends to get the new furniture."

"You sure have done a great job in such a short time. Now let's go see the rest of the house." Mama praised Baba; she was quite pleased with the place.

We walked through the three bedrooms. Again, two of them were fully furnished. There was even furniture in the living room. I was given the smaller private bedroom.

"May I go outside and look around now?" I asked Baba, since I had no interest to inspect other parts of the house immediately. I wanted to explore the surroundings.

"Sure, just be careful not to venture into the mountainside. People told me there are dangerous objects around the foot of the mountain area," said Baba.

"I will be careful, Baba," I said. I rushed out of the door, walked to the beach, and quickly looked over the surrounding areas. This was truly the most beautiful place I had ever been. Better than any tourist attractions I had seen in the past. In fact, I never thought such a beautiful place existed. I was so happy that we came to Taiwan instead of Kwangchow or any other city on the mainland.

Our house was about two hundred yards from the white sand beach on the west coast of southern Taiwan. At the north end of the beach, about two hundred yards from the compound, on a cliff overlooking the bay, was the white mansion where President Chiang Kai Sheik resided when he visited south Taiwan for a short stay. There were plenty of ancient giant banyan trees and tropical flowers all over the entire area. The banyan tree is a native tree of southern Taiwan. It likes the subtropical weather and can live for a thousand years. At the center of the park on open ground, between the compound and the white mansion, was this giant banyan with its surface root spreading over a hundred square feet and shading an area four times the size of its surface root. The surface root of the banyan served as benches for adults and a playground for kids.

The shoreline was a pristine beach and a stretch of land unspoiled by tourist crowds or overdevelopment. Its clean, grayish-white sand beach stretched about two miles long. To the north, the shoreline became rocky and very steep. To the south, a mile-long concrete wave barrier intersected the sandy beach. A road along the side of the rocky shoreline leading to the southern tip at the foot of the Sou Mountain led to the city. The entire beach was not accessible by civilians and was mostly empty throughout the day. The regular users of the beach were the few teenage kids of the military dependents living in the compound. Occasionally, two or three times a year, the beach would be opened to the public on Sundays. When it was open to the public, the beach would be crowded with people from all over the island. When it was open, armed guards would be stationed at strategic points around the beach.

The mountains behind the beach were hidden with unknown numbers of the big eighteen-inch shore defense cannons overlooking the harbor and the strait that divides the mainland and Taiwan. Because there was the serious threat of a Red Army invasion, the security on the island was extremely tight. Armed guards were ordered to shoot any unauthorized person prowling anywhere in the entire restricted area.

I was so happy that the rumors we heard in Fu-Chow about Taiwan could not be farther from the truth. Not only there was enough food for the population and the flood of military and civilians from the mainland, it had a surplus of rice to export to other nations. Looking at the people and houses, I could tell that the economy in Taiwan was far stronger than that on the mainland. Most importantly, we no longer had the constant fear of underground among us in Taiwan. We now could talk normally in our home, on the street, and in public places. People traded confidently with the Taiwan currency that would not depreciate its value like the gold certificate on the mainland. Not only that, my parents and I were safe and well. But most of all, we could live together every day. Baba went to work in the morning and came home for dinner every evening—a normal family life that was a rare thing in my family when we were on the mainland. I also felt so blessed and fortunate to live right in the paradise-like place during my teen years. What more one could ask for?

The weather in the fall of southern Taiwan was just ideal. It would rain before dawn and be sunny the rest of the day during the first few days after our arrival. When I woke up each morning, I was so taken by the clean air and the crisp, bright, and colorful surroundings. I appreciated our residence that was well built with wood and plaster and a cured-clay roof. The house was complete with electric outlets and plenty of lights. Because the weather was very mild year-round, there was no heating or air-conditioning needed in the house. One constant companion in the house with us was the "wall tigers" (geckos). The geckos were small lizards that could walk on the wall. They changed color to match the environment. Since the house was new, the wall tigers were all in white. They chirped loudly all the time. It took a while for me to get used to the noise. They also did a good service for us—catching and eating flies and mosquitoes. No one was ever bitten by a wall tiger anywhere in Taiwan.

A week after our arrival, Captain Li came to our house and brought the two small suitcases from our house in Fu-chow.

"I went to your home to see your mother two days after you and Tien-Ren left Fu-chow," Captain Li told Mama. "She was sad but understood you had to sneak away under the watchful eyes of the underground. She wanted me to tell you not to worry about her."

"How was Fu-Chow after we left?" asked Mama.

"Not much different when we left a week later, but we heard the Red army was getting closer to Fu-chow at that time."

"What about my dad? Is he going to come?" Mama still worried about Wye Gong.

"Uh! I was going to tell you. I arranged to put him on a ship leaving Fu-chow soon. He may show up here any day now," Captain Li said with a big smile.

"Really!" Mama exclaimed, tears rolling down her eyes—the tears of joy. I was very happy too to see Wye Gong again.

"We have an empty room here. He can stay with us, right, Mama?" I asked.

"Of course, Wye Gong will stay with us. I will get his room ready before he arrives." Mama was very happy.

When Baba heard about Wye Gong coming, he said he was pleased too. Three days later, Wye Gong did arrive at our house. Surprisingly, he brought two large suitcases with him. In the suitcases were items we could not take with us plus some items he had selected from the library. Baba was most appreciative that he had again received those treasured books left by Yeh-Yeh.

"You know I was among the last few to leave Fu-Chow. It was very chaotic and scary because people said the Red Army was within hours to enter Fu-Chow. Since I am just a nobody old man, the Communists did not bother me at all when I left the pier," Wye Gong told us as he rested on the sofa and drank hot tea.

"Wye Gong, did you come with the troops on the ship?" I was curious.

"I sure did, and there were no other ships taking passengers."

"When did you and other people find out Mama and I sneaked out of Fu-chow?"

"When you did not show up after ten that night, Wye Po panicked. That was the first time in years she talked to me and asked me to help. Because she thought you two might be harmed on the street," Wye Gong said with a smile. He sipped his tea. "I went to the police precinct. They had not heard any report. So, I went to see Captain Li at his home. He told me you were all safe and on your way to Taiwan. When I told him I also wanted to leave Fu-Chow, he immediately promised me to make the arrangement. I then went back to tell your Wye Po that you are safe. She was much relieved."

"Did all of people who wanted to leave got out?" I asked a dumb question.

"Not at all. Many people did not even know where to go, and the ones who wanted to come to Taiwan just could not find any means of transportation. If Captain Li did not help me, I would still be in Fu-chow now," said Wye Gong.

By the time Wye Gong came to our house, Fu-Chow was already occupied by the Red Army. We had heard the broadcast from the Central People's Broadcast on August 27, 1949, that Fu-chow was liberated by the Red Army, but the newspaper and broadcast TV never mentioned a word about it until sometime later. Baba told me the Red Army continued its drive down south and the west. The Nationalists still had many troops and officials in Chunking and surrounding area. Some of them would be evacuated to Taiwan soon. The evacuation of troops and war material continued in Kwang-Dong Province. Ships carrying soldiers, weapons, and ammunition came in the harbor daily. I knew in my heart that soon the mainland would be completely lost to the Red Army.

The government told the people in Taiwan that we will retake the mainland after taking a break from the war to regroup. At the meantime, we just settled down to enjoy the peaceful, stable, and more prosperous life on this beautiful island.

CHAPTER 2

EXPLOSION IN THE HARBOR

We arrived at our new home on August 7, 1949. By August 27, Fu-Chow was lost, and by the end of August, the entire Fujian Province was "liberated." The ships for evacuation from other parts of the mainland still came and unloaded in the harbor. I watched the ships on the beach and wondered when the last ship would come from the mainland.

One day, at about ten in the morning, I was listening to the radio broadcast at home. A tremendous boom came from the direction of the city. While the house was still shaking from the first boom, the second, third and other explosions followed. Was it the Red Army bombardment of the city? Or was it the air raid from their air force? Suddenly the whole world crumbled in my mind. We had just settled into this peaceful paradise and now the war had followed us here! I rushed to the yard in front of the house and saw the thick black smoke rise hundreds of feet from the southern part of the city. In a few minutes, the explosion had stopped but blackened debris and dust of unknown substance fell all over the whole area and the compound.

"Mama, do you think we are attacked by the Red Army?" I asked when Mama came out of the house.

"I don't know. It is scary," Mama was shaken from the explosion as well. Her lips were white and visibly trembling.

"Mama, if it is bombing, how come the bombs only fall on one spot? I think the smoke is only from one area and the explosion has stopped so quickly." I tried to analyze the situation.

"It might be an ammo dump or something like that exploded." Mrs. Lu who lived two houses down joined Mama and the others.

"It makes sense to me," Mama said. "The Red Air Force has no planes that can break through our air defense to begin with. Besides, why would they just bomb one spot in the city?"

We concluded that the explosion was an accident and not the Red attack. Feeling more assured, we brushed the dust and debris off our heads and clothing. It was a mess trying to clean our faces and hands from the black, smelly, and sticky substance. I was much relieved to know we were not under any enemy attack, at least for now.

At lunchtime, Baba came home to check on us.

"Baba, what was that explosion? It was so loud and so messy," I said.

"The ship transporting bombs and cannon shells from Hainan Island exploded on the pier when workers were unloading the ammunition. I have only the preliminary report, but I should know more this evening," Baba said with a very serious look on his face. I knew the security of the city was the responsibility of the Shore Defense Command. Baba was directly involved with this incident. After a quick lunch, Baba went back to his office.

That afternoon, I spent much of the time talking with my new friends in the compound about the horrific explosion. Ru-Kao, a few months younger, was about my height of five feet, four inches. Yu-Si, same age as me, was about six feet tall. And Tsang-Mou, a year younger than us, was only five feet, one inch tall.

"Does anybody know what has happened to the ammunition ship?" Ru-Kao asked.

"I think the Red spies have set up time charges to damage our supplies of our vital ammunition for our defense," Tsang-Mou said.

"In that case, do you mean they are preparing to attack us following the destruction of our ammunition supplies?" Yu-Si asked.

"That makes sense. Otherwise why would they go to the trouble to destroy our ammunition?" Ru-Kao theorized.

"But we really don't know how bad the damage was and what was blown up," Tsang-Mou said. "I would like to see it for myself. How about let's go to the pier and see the explosion site?"

"I don't think we can go. I heard the entire city is under curfew. You must have a pass to get close to the pier and then I know for sure we can't get near where the ship is tied up," Ru-Kao said. We went home separately after we had exhausted all we could imagine about what had really happened.

That evening, Baba came home later than usual and was exhausted. I did not want to bother him before dinner. After dinner, Mama made a large pot of his favorite black tea and helped him light his cigarette. Baba sat on the sofa and Wye Gong sat in a chair next to his hot tea mug. Both were relaxing in the living room. I saw they were in good mood, so I pulled up a stool, sat near Baba, and tried to find out more about the explosion.

"Baba, are you too tired to talk to me?" I asked.

"I am fine," he said as he sipped a big mouthful of the hot tea. "You want to know about the ammo ship, right?"

"Yes, Baba, what has happened? Was it sabotage by Red spies?" I couldn't wait for his answer.

"No. It was not sabotaged by anyone. It was a bad accident. A fire had started in the engine room and then ignited a fuel storage tank. People tried to put the fire out, but it spread to other compartments. Unfortunately, the cargo on that ship was too heavy to be removed in time. The explosion came too quickly. All the people on board and many people in the nearby buildings and ships were killed or wounded. I don't know how many casualties we have currently. It is a real mess." Baba sighed.

"Have you been at the site yourself?" Wye Gong asked.

"I sure have been at the site briefly this afternoon. It is bad. You know the entire number 2 pier has disappeared. All the buildings nearby are flattened. You and your mother landed here on that pier just couple of weeks ago," Baba said, looking at my direction briefly.

"It is gone, the whole place?" I exclaimed, because that was a big pier with a large concrete lot for staging and loading. There were many offices, maintenance shops, and storage buildings around the pier. "May I go see it tomorrow?"

"You can't get close to the place if you go. But maybe I can take you with me tomorrow morning," Baba said.

"Can I go too?" Wye Gong had curiosity too, at the ancient age of sixty. I thought people at such advanced age would not be so curious!

"Sure, tomorrow you both come to my office at nine o'clock. We will go from there," Baba said. He inhaled the smoke deep into his lung and slowly puffed into the air.

The next morning, Wye Gong and I walked the twenty minutes from our house through the tunnel and to the back of the Sou Mountain where the Shore Defense Command headquarters was located. We waited in the front of the lobby for about five minutes. Baba came out with his assistant, Major Huang. We hopped onto a Jeep. Major Huang drove us through the winding streets and through several checkpoints to the pier. Armed guards were everywhere. On the Jeep was a small flag on the fender so we did not stop at any of the checkpoints. As we approached the vicinity of the pier, it was just unbelievable. In front of us were those charred, and smoldering collapsed buildings, the torn-apart ships, and the whole number 2 pier simply disappeared.

Hundreds of workers and soldiers were hard at work digging and moving debris. An awfully strong stench filled the air. Bodies dug out of the rubbles were carried away in stretchers.

"Search for survivors was over last night. We didn't believe we could find anyone still alive by night fall," a supervisor of the working group, stopped by Major Huang, told us. "I believe bodies of some victims are still buried under the rubles, so we don't know what the total number of the casualties yet."

"Where is the ship?" I asked, because in front where the pier used to be there was no site of a damaged ship.

"The ship was demolished, and the broken pieces are in the water," Major Huang said, pointing the direction of the sunken ship. "Several ships nearby were either damaged or sunk but we are unable to determine the number of ships destroyed, damaged, or sunk at this time."

We spent only about twenty minutes at the scene and left depressed. We rode the Jeep back where we came from. Along the way, I found many of the stores and vendors near the pier were burned down. I felt heartsick to see some of those shops selling electronic parts and devices were among the shops destroyed by the explosion.

"It is a shame to have those electronic surplus shops burned down," I said.

"There are many of them in the city. Everywhere you go, you will find them. This is only a very small part of the surplus business here. If you make a left turn instead of turning right in front of the tunnel, that will take you to the biggest concentration of surplus stores," Major Huang told me.

"Thank you, Uncle Huang, for telling me this." I was truly happy to hear that there were other surplus shops in the city.

Baba dropped us at the entrance of the tunnel. Wye Gong and I walked back to the house while Baba and Major Huang drove back to the Shore Defense Headquarters.

"I had seen a lot of destructions in Manchuria after the Japanese had attacked the cities, but there was nothing like this," Wye Gong told me.

"Well, the bomb damages to the air raid shelters in Chunking were very extensive as well, but yesterday there were over fifty thousand tons of bombs on the ship exploded at one time. It is like the power of two 20KT atomic bombs exploded at Pier 2 but without radiation," I said.

"I don't think it is as powerful as a 20KT atomic bomb. A 20KT atomic bomb like the one dropped on Hiroshima would flatten the whole city of Kao-Shiung, right?" Wye Gong corrected me.

"I guess you are right, but still this is a horrific explosion," I said.

"Well, it is a great tragedy. I am very sad that we have lost many lives and the pier, but I am relieved that this was not a hostile action carried out by our enemies and was just an accident," Wye Gong said.

I gathered my friends in the compound and briefed them on what I had seen at the explosion site because none of them had the chance to see the site.

"The whole pier 2 is not there anymore. Houses on the street near the pier are also burned up. I tell you the smell is horrible," I said. "My dad told me it is not a case of sabotage or air raid. It is an accident on the ammunition ship." What I told them was so anticlimactic that all seemed a bit disappointed.

"Oh! Well, accidents happen every day. We are too far away for the Communists' navy or air force to attack us. I am not worried," Yu-Si said.

"True, our navy can stop them when they try to cross the Taiwan Strait. I don't think they have any air force to speak of. I heard that we would counterattack the mainland when we get all of our troops and equipment over here and retrain them," Ru-Kao said.

"That makes sense. I have counted at least four or five big ships come in the harbor every day. I believe those are the ships from Kwan-Dong and southern Fujian provinces," Yu-Si said.

The official report came out on the newspaper the next morning saying there were over three hundred people—civilians and soldiers—killed and many more were wounded. No word was mentioned about what had caused the explosion. The area was off limits to traffic and no civilians could enter the area while the investigation and cleaning up work continued.

Life went on uneventfully for the rest of the week. People soon stopped talking about the explosion. The attention of the few of us turned to schools that we were going to attend, since all of us had just come from the mainland. This island was a curiosity to all people from the mainland. Now we were quite curious about how the schools were like in Kao-Shiung. I was praying they would not be anything like the temple school in rural Chunking.

"Which school are you going to attend?" I asked Ru-Kao, who had been here a few more days than all of us.

The Island Heaven

"I am not sure. How about let's go look at both the provincial and the city high schools?" Ru-Kao suggested. The four of us agreed to take a quick tour that afternoon. We left the compound, walked out the tunnel, and bought bus tickets from this tiny magazine stand. The number 3 bus would take us to the railroad station at the north end of the city, where it was close to the provincial high school.

The bus made frequent stops but still arrived at the railroad station in twenty-five minutes. There would be another ten-minute walk to get to the school. The Japanese-built school was very large and impressive to all of us. We tried to walk inside the gate but were turned back by school guards because we were not students there. We then walked for about thirty minutes to reach the city high school, which was in the midway of the bus route between the tunnel and Provincial High School. The city high school was much smaller and less impressive; therefore, our goal was to enter the provincial high school. But the registration and entrance test would not be administrated for another week or later.

There were about twenty-five children in the compound; ten of them were about my age of fifteen years old. Every kid in the compound spoke Mandarin or Chunking dialect but not Taiwanese. My best friends in the compound were Ru-Kao Chang, Yu-Si Tsao, and Tsang-Mou Liao. All of them were a few months younger than me. A week after touring the school, we went to the schools and applied for entrance. A two-day entrance examination was given. I was accepted to the provincial high as the second-semester ninth grader. Yu-Si was accepted in the seventh grade. Ru-Kao and Tzun-Mou were accepted to the city high as eighth and seventh graders. The day after the school started, Yu-Si came to me almost in tears.

"The admissions people want the diploma of my elementary school. I told him I did not bring it with us in a hurry when we escaped the mainland. He told me I must turn it in and there will be no exceptions. It is just unreasonable," Yu-Si told me. That reminded me of my situation at Chun-Nan High School three years ago.

"Can you ask your dad to take you to see the principal of the school and explain to them the problem?" I suggested.

"My dad is in Chunking right now. I don't even know when he will come to Taiwan." Yu-Si was desperate, so I thought I could use my experience learned from Kwan-Yu.

"All right, I know a way to get around, but it is illegal. Do you mind?"

"I don't care if it's illegal as long as I could get through this obstacle," said Yu-Si.

"If you don't mind doing, then I will show you how to make a diploma yourself," I told him. "You write the diploma with your school name and your name plus all of the specifics."

"But where do I get the school seal? They all have a seal on it."

"That's easy. You just get a piece of dry soap, carve out some impression, and just put a lot of ink on it. No one can tell the difference," I said confidently.

"You talk as if you have done it before!"

"As a matter of fact, I did when I was going into the seventh grade in Chunking."

"Please help me, since you have the experience," he pleaded.

"Now you know if we get caught, we will all be in big trouble. You have to swear you will not tell people where you learned about this." I was concerned because he talked a lot with friends.

"I swear!" He raised his three fingers as a scout symbol.

"All right let's get a sample diploma and copy it word for word except the names and dates. Can you borrow one from someone?" I asked.

"Sure, I can borrow one from my sister. She just graduated from a junior high school in Nanking before we came here," said Yu-Si.

That evening, Yu-Si came to my house. We copied the diploma with his name and his school's name on it. Then we made a crude seal and chopped the diploma with a blob of red ink. Yu-Si went home quite relieved, but I was sweating. The next morning, we went to school together. I insisted to go to the admissions office to turn the fake diploma in because I was not comfortable with Yu-Si's ability to deal with the clerk in the office.

"Don't be nervous. I will be with you all the way. Just answer any questions calmly," I assured him.

When we walked in the office, I saw the man in charge of the records office was a young man in the twenties. He took the diploma and stared at Yu-Si for a few second with a strange smile.

"Where are you from? You look very familiar to me, but I can't place where have we met before," the young man said.

"I am from Hu-Pei. My dad is the representative from that province," Yu-Si said, still sweating.

"Oh, yes, I think I saw you when we were on the same ship. You were with your sister then," he said as he put the fake diploma in a folder. I didn't think he even looked at it. Yu-Si came out with sweat running down his forehead.

"I thought I was going to have a heart attack when he put up that screwy smile. My god, I am so glad it's over," Yu-Si said as he wiped his sweat on his forehead with his short sleeves. I knew exactly what he felt. I was in the same situation three years ago.

CHAPTER 3

VENTURES IN THE PARADISE

Two weeks after we moved into the new house, I couldn't contain my urge to visit the many electronic surplus vendors on the streets in the city.

"Mama, I would like to go to the city to see the electronics stores. May I?" I expected a rejection.

"All right, you may go, but be very careful. Here is a one-dollar Taiwan bill. Keep it in your pocket just in case you are hungry." Mama knew I had to see the "junk," as she termed those radios and electronic parts.

"Thank you, Mama. I will be back in just a few hours." I was very excited about what I might find on the trip to town.

I proceeded alone, walking the two to three miles of street to find the electronics vendors that Major Huang had told me about. I walked along the residential alleys and commercial streets in this new city, observing the different building styles and general environment. I felt good walking leisurely on the cement sidewalks along nice and neat Japanese-style houses. After walking for about thirty minutes, I did find a street full of such junk stores and roadside vendors. The stores were very small, about twelve feet wide and less than twenty feet deep. There must have been twenty-five such stores. In front of the stores and on the sidewalks, there were many one-person vendors displaying their goods on the cement floor or on a small table. It was a wonderland for me. I saw all sorts of meters, motors, chassis, vacuum tubes, radio sets, and partially assembled electronic equipment.

Many Japanese World War II military radios and personal items were on display on the block of a small street. Some vendors were specialized in American surplus equipment—mostly electronic parts and partial equipment discarded after the war. I had never seen just about any of those items before, except a few broken parts I picked up from the two crashed planes. I lingered on, inspecting item after item, for several hours before I reluctantly left the area and returned home. Because I had not had enough money in my pocket, I did not even ask for prices. I could have bought a truckload of them home if I had the money.

Inside the compound, everyone spoke Mandarin, but once on the street, the local people all spoke Taiwanese. I could not speak a word of it, although I could speak northern Fujian dialect. Once we left the tunnel, the environment would turn unfriendly and occasionally it even became hostile. The next day, I asked Mama for some money to buy some electronics parts.

"I want to build a crystal radio. May I have ten dollars today?" I asked. Ten dollars in Taiwan money was not much money at the time.

"Crystal radio is fine. Just don't bring too much junk home. We don't have that much space in the house for that. Here is fifteen dollars for you. Use it wisely now." Mama had always been generous on my allowance.

"Thank you, Mama. I will be back before lunch," I said. I rushed out of the door and proceeded to the surplus street I had visited the day before. I first bought some enamel wires for the coil and then a set of American-made military earphones. The next thing I needed was a crystal. I could not find a Chinese medicine store around there, so I walked into a surplus store. In the store was a man in his thirties. When he saw me walking toward him, he started to cuss in the Taiwanese dialect. I could not understand most of what he said, but I could tell it was very bad language, mostly foul words. I could see fire come out of his eyes and his veins on his head visibly swelled. It scared me so much I backed out of the store in a hurry. I was trying to find out why he was so mad at me. I knew for sure I had never met him in the past and I had not done anything to provoke him—strange! I determined that he was not mad at me as a person. Depressed, I went home without finishing my shopping list. That evening, after dinner, when Baba was relaxing with his hot tea and cigarettes, I went to find out from Baba.

"Baba, I was in a store to buy parts. A Taiwanese storeowner acted like a crazy man. I thought he was going to kill me," I reported.

"What did you do to provoke him?" asked Baba.

"Nothing. I walked into the store before talking to him and he just exploded in anger and cussed me. I don't understand."

"Well, son, I think it's time you learn something of the past of the local people." Baba took a deep puff and drank a big mouthful of the hot tea. "There had been some very unfortunate events before we came here."

"May I join in to listen?" Wye Gong pulled up a chair and sat next to me.

"Of course, Daddy. After the Japanese repatriated Taiwan to our government in 1946, the locals were very happy to be freed from the Japanese as the second-class citizens and become citizens of China again. What happened was the first bunch of officials sent by Nanjing government was very bad—corrupted and treated Taiwan people badly. They would take away homes and properties from the people. When the local people protested, the commanding general ordered soldiers to suppress the crowd.

The situation soon worsened when soldiers opened fire on a group of protesters marching through the main street of Kao-Shiung. At end of the day, scores of people were killed and wounded. The government immediately posted martial law. Soldiers went to people's house in the name of searching for riot inciters and committed several unspeakable crimes that really made the mainlanders an enemy to the locals, even worse than the Japanese occupation. When President

Chiang moved to Taiwan in 1948, he discovered what was going on. An investigation found many high-ranking officials responsible for the killing of innocent people. Several were executed, others were jailed, but the hate toward the mainlander was deeply rooted." Baba spoke with a big sigh.

"I see. No wonder the storeowner was so mad at me just because I am a mainlander. This is very sad indeed," I said.

"I really feel bad for the local people. I wish the Nanjing government had sent some smarter people in 1947. We would all be happier today," Wye Gong said.

"When you lose the heart of the people, you lose the country. Fortunately, the government realized this basic principle. They have started the so-called 375 rental act that reduced the rental fee for farmers a year ago. This has made the farmers very happy. As you know, 80 percent of the local people on this island are farmers," Baba said. Again, he gulped down more hot tea and had a deep puff of his cigarette. "I hope from now on, the relationship between the mainlander and the locals will improve. After all, we were all from the mainland."

"We just learned a big lesson on the mainland. Didn't we?" Wye Gong agreed. "It is good that we have won the hearts of the majority people, the farmers, here."

"How about people in the cities, on the street, and in the shops? We have to deal with them all the time." I was very concerned, especially for those people in surplus stores.

"Well, I believe things will improve. It has been very calm in the last few months. When we are ready, we will counterattack and regain the mainland. At that time, we will all return to our homes on the mainland," Baba said confidently. I was hoping Baba was right. On the other hand, I really liked to stay longer on this beautiful island.

I was just two months past my fifteenth birthday when we arrived at Taiwan in August 1949. Like all my friends at this age, we thought we knew everything there was to know under the sun. We thought our parents were overprotective and old-fashioned. We all had good plans for ourselves. First, we thought sixteen was a threshold for us to cross as a kid to a man. I especially wanted to treasure every minute of my time at the age fifteen. Yu-Si was two months younger than I was, and he also had the same feelings.

"Yu-Si, what do you think is the most important thing we want to do before we turn sixteen?" I wanted to hear what he had to say, because he was very smart in social activities and seemed to know a lot of philosophy in life—I thought.

"Well, of course you want to develop your body before you get too old," he said.

"What do you mean by developing my body?"

"Look at your arms. You don't have any muscles there, do you?"

"No. I sure don't have much, but what do you suggest?"

"Have you seen the Joe Louis movies? Did you see his muscles on his arms? That is the basic requirement to become a world boxing champion. If you want to be a strong man, you need to prepare for it now." He sure seemed to know what he was talking about and believed he was right.

"How about we do it together? What do you think we need to do?"

"Well, you heard about the weightlifting, right?" he asked, and I said yes.

"The first thing to do is to find something for us to practice weight- lifting," he said.

"All right, how about let's look around near the mountainside? There is so much stuff left there by the Japanese," I suggested.

"Well, what else do we wait for? Let's go and see what we can find!" he urged.

We took off from my house and walked quickly to the back of the compound. The treed mountainside was just a hundred feet away from the back of the compound. We walked along the wild-growth-covered light railroad track toward the north. Along the track, many rusty metal objects and rotted wooden boxes littered about. After ten minutes of walking and looking, we arrived at an area with rusted and abandoned rail cars and some cars with side panels missing.

"Look at the rail car wheels. It would be ideal if we can find one to use as the dumb bells," I said.

"If we look hard enough, we will find one that is loose." Yu-Si kept moving forward next to me. When we saw several sets of the wheels on the side of the track yards away, my heart almost jumped out of my chest with joy.

"See the wheels there? This is from heaven!" Yu-Si exclaimed. He rushed to the few wheels randomly lying in the grass. We tried to lift one off the ground. It was so heavy I could only hold it for a few second before dropping it back on the ground.

"I say it weighs over sixty pounds. What do you think?" I asked.

"It is more than one hundred pounds, I think." He was still puffing from trying to lift the wheels. I judged the wheel with the axle at one and a half inches in diameter and the two twelve-inch wheels on each end were about fifty to sixty pounds. It was too heavy for me to lift above my head, but if I practiced enough, I should be able to make it someday.

"How about help me to move one to my home?" I asked.

"You are crazy! This is too heavy for us to do lifting. If we can find one without the wheels on it, that will really be ideal," Yu-Si insisted.

"Well, I really want to make it a goal to lift the wheel above my head like those athletes do in school. Will you help me?" I pleaded because I could not bring this wheel home alone.

"All right, I will give you a hand, but I still think you are crazy. And don't blame me when you get hurt," Yu-Si muttered.

"Nobody will get hurt from this, and I promise I will be careful," I assured him.

The two of us got hold of the wheel on each end and struggled to walk the two hundred yards or so on the rough path to bring that wheel to my home. We put it on the side of our front yard, right beside my bedroom windows.

"What are you doing with that rusty thing?" Mama came out of the house and asked me.

"I am going to use it to exercise weightlifting for my muscles," I answered.

"I thought those crab claws you eat are supposed to grow your muscle." Mama teased me about the countless raw crab claws I caught in the stream back in rural Chunking.

"Mama, this exercise will build my muscles on my arms. You'll see."

That afternoon, I cleaned the rusty wheel with steel brush and rough sandpaper. It turned out quite nice. Tired, I did not do any lifting that evening, but I dreamed about the weightlifting and my muscle building all night. I dreamed I fell on my back and struggled to get up and fell again when I tried to lift it above my head. I also dreamed my arms and shoulders had muscles like that of Mr. Universe. I woke up early the next morning to check on the wheels. Without delay, I lifted it off the ground and put it down repeatedly five times. That amount of effort was enough to make me feel exhausted. I planned to increase the number of lifts little by little each day, but the first few days, my arms and legs were so painful, I had to rub muscle ointment on my muscles to ease the pain. In about a week, I was able to pick the wheels up with ease. When Yu-Si saw me lifting it so easily, he couldn't believe it, but he still refused to try.

I went to observe people weightlifting at the city gym and learned the way they lift weight over their heads. Two weeks later, I tried to lift the wheel to my shoulder level by using the jerking motion. On the first two or three tries, it almost threw me backward to the ground, and that had the danger of crashing my ribs or skull. Fortunately, no one else had seen that hair-raising moment. I finally learned how to lift to my shoulder height without tipping over. Now the challenge was to push it above my head. I decided to do the shoulder height for a week then try the push it above my head. Surprisingly it was much easier than the stage of lifting to shoulder height. I threw down the wheels on the ground and ran into the house to find Mama.

"Mama come out and see this," I said.

"What is going on now?" Mama came out of the house anyway. I did the whole sequence of lifting to knee high, jerking up to the shoulder, and pushing the wheels above my head. Mama stood there astonished to see what I had done.

"Son, it is too heavy and dangerous. I am scared the thing would drop on your head." Mama looked very worried about it.

"Mama, this wheel is only sixty pounds. It is not dangerous at all. Please don't worry. Look. I will show you how easy it is," I said, and I did the sequence again. "See? I am not even tired and look at my arms." I showed Mama my bulging muscles.

"All right, son. Please don't overdo it and be very careful. It may bust your lung if you try too hard." Mama seemed to feel more relaxed after I assured her that I would be very, very careful when I did the weightlifting.

Yu-Si never wanted to touch the wheels, but he was consistent with our morning of jogging and simple exercises. Each morning I always got up around six. After cleaning up, I would go to Yu-Si's home, tapping on his window to wake him up. We then jogged along the shore to the south end guard post and back to the compound, where we would do some stationary exercises.

"Yu-Si, come with me to do some weightlifting." I tried to entice him to try the wheels out almost every day.

"No, I don't think so. You know your body and brain development at this time is like the same amount of water divided into two cups. If one cup has more water, the other one will have less. I am worried you will end up a muscleman but not enough up there," Yu-Si said with his finger pointing to his head.

"Where in the world did you learn that from? As far as I know, the healthier and stronger you are, your brain will function better too," I argued.

"Well, my friend, you are a very stubborn man. I have tried to advise you, but you will not listen to me. It is your life," Yu-Si said. He left me alone to do the lifting.

I really did not take him seriously because since I started the weightlifting, I felt better physically, and my head seemed even clearer after a good workout with the wheels. Soon the weight of the wheel was too light for me, so I added some odds and ends of metal to each end the wheel. My shoulder was so full of muscle that I could not even feel the shoulder bones when I tried to find them with my hand. All the exercises were done before the other kids got out of their beds. As days went by, we all grew taller and stronger, but no one knew why I had developed my muscle so well, and nobody bothered to find out either.

On the third week since we arrived in Taiwan, something was dreadfully wrong. That was in the evening when we were eating supper. Suddenly, the house was swinging, the wood joints were making loud squeaky noise, the lights went out, and the room was warbling. Caught by surprise, I thought the whole world was going to collapse and come down on us.

"Go quickly to the open yard. We have an earthquake," Baba said. Dropping our chopsticks, we all ran out to the open yard, where many people were already there. Out in the yard, I still felt the earth was moving under my feet, as if we were on a boat in the ocean.

"This is a big earthquake, isn't it?" Mrs. Shao said as she trembled.

"No, not really. Taiwan has earthquakes every day. Most of them are so light you do not even feel them. This is a medium one we have just now. It might be over soon, and it may have aftershocks and follow-up quakes. I have seen so many of them in the last year. This one is harmless," said an officer of the Shore Defense Command.

After staying outside for about thirty minutes, people started to calm down and return to their homes. We continued to finish our supper in the dark. The lights never came back until the next day. The next night as I was ready to fall asleep, the light bulb in my bedroom was swinging slowly, but the house joints didn't make any noise. I knew then that earthquakes in this island haven were common and frequent. I just had to get used to them. The paradise was not always hospitable to its inhabitants.

Before the school started, we had all kinds of free time. To all the kids in the compound, this was a very exciting place to explore, because the Japanese used this location as the Shore Defense Command, and when they fled, they left a large amount of materials scattered around the mountainside, and some were hidden in caves made by the Japanese. Because the newly arrived troops had other important tasks to do, no one paid any attention to the unknown materials left by the Japanese. To me, that was a very exciting idea

The Island Heaven

to explore the unknown. I imagined all sorts of things the Japanese might have left in the area: radios, telephones, binoculars, or even weapons.

On a bright August morning, the four of us had gathered under that cool shade of the giant banyan tree, as we had done almost every day after breakfast.

"How about let's go to the mountainside to explore and see if we can find some treasures left by the Japanese or the bandits?" I suggested.

"I wouldn't go near the mountainside. People said there are snakes if thirty feet in this tropical forest. One of them can eat us all," Tsang-Mou said.

"Nonsense. That kind of snake can only be found in India or Burma, not here. Besides, my dad said the Japanese had eradicated the poisonous snakes when they were here, and the local people are catching them for snake soup too," Ru-Kao said.

"Well, with the fighting power of the four of us, we are not even afraid of a tiger, and if we equip ourselves with machetes and slingshots, we can face any danger there is." I tried to encourage the two less venturous fellows: Tsang-Mou and Yu-Si.

"All right, I will go," Yu-Si said. "But we need to go home to get our weapons."

"I will go too," Tsang-Mou said.

"That is great. Let us meet at the east end of the compound in ten minutes. How is that?" I asked. The three agreed and we headed for our homes to fetch "weapons."

The local folklore claimed that giant and poisonous snakes and other harmful animals were hidden in the forest and were ready to attack people when people entered their hideouts. But the curiosity in us had overcome the unproven stories. So, armed with slingshots and a machete, I led the three brave souls into the mountainside forest behind the housing complex.

We were very cautious but not really scared as we walked into the darkened forest. We walked in single file, slowly climbing the vine-infested and bushy slope. I was leading the group climbing the mild slope straightforward, without any inclination of what were we might see. Ru-Kao, Yu-Si, and Tsang-Mou followed in that order. Everybody was concentrating on any moving thing, but the strange and new place kept us very busy.

Nothing threatening showed up. A few small monkeys high on the trees were barking at us, and a few giant lizards bobbed their heads on the trees ahead of us. So far, we had not seen a snake or any big animal. Even Tsan-Mou was relaxed after a while.

One hundred yards or so onto the side slope of the mountain, we found a wide path crossing in front of us, though it was filled with wild growth. With the heavy growth on it, apparently no one had walked on it for a long while. Suddenly, Tsang-Mou jumped off his feet and ran toward the three of us in the front.

"Look there! A snake on the tree!" He pointed to the tree on the left and behind us.

"It is not a snake! I think it is just another kind of lizard with its head looking like a snake. Just look at the legs." Ru-Kao laughed and Tsan-Mou was a bit embarrassed.

"Which way should we go now?" Ru-Kao asked.

"Let's make a right turn here and mark where we came from, so we will not get lost," I said, then we walked south for about thirty feet.

"Look! Isn't it an entrance of a cave?" Tsang-Mou exclaimed, pointing toward the mountainside on our left.

"Let's take a closer look," I said. I led the way, approaching the area through the thick vines and undergrowth among tall trees.

"It is a cave!" Tsang-Mou called out. That was indeed a cave entrance the size of a double door gate. It could only be seen in close range and with great concentration; otherwise, it would be easily missed. Years of wild growth had covered the entrance with layers of vines and bushes.

"We can't go in unless we bring some large machetes to chop out the vines and bushes," I told the group, because the small machete we had carried would never be able to chop off the massive inch-thick vines.

"It is going to be a lot hard work to open up enough room for us to go through the cave opening," Ru-Kao said. "Let's get ready and start now. I will go home and get my dad's machete. Yu-Si, why don't you get one from your home too? I think we need them to chop out these thick vines if we want to get in there," Ru-Kao said to Yu-Si as he swung his arms like he was chopping a tree.

"Ru-Kao, would you bring a flashlight too? I think we'll need all of the lights we can get to see anything inside the cave," I said.

"All right, I will get a flashlight. Anything else?" he asked me before he turned around and quickly walked toward where we came from.

"Don't tell any other fellows about this. We don't know if this was the treasure hidden by pirates!" Tsang-Mou looked said. "I don't want to share with those guys who are not here with us today."

In his mind, he must see the glittering chest full of gold. The way he acted so seriously; I knew he was not joking. After he finished talking to me, he left for home with Ru-Kao and Yu-Si to get tools. I stayed at the cave entrance, using the small machete to chop down the smaller undergrowth. I was very excited to find out what might be in this old cave too. Not so much of the gold and jewelry but a weapons cache, which was more logical! As I looked around, I saw some foot-long lizards running about the bushes and vines, but they were trying to stay out of my way. I felt much better when there was no snake in sight near the cave, but I was still on guard just in case there were some hidden in the bushes.

In about fifteen minutes, the three came back with two large machetes and two flashlights. We began taking turns to chop the vines and the small tree-like growth. It was much harder than we had anticipated. The inch-thick vines were very tough, and there was not enough room to swing the machete. For some tough old vines, it would take at least ten minutes to cut just one of them, and a lot were intertwined at about a foot or so deep in front of the cave. We worked for at least two hours before we could open enough space for us to squeeze into the cave, one at a time.

I entered the cave first, and the other kids followed. Luckily, we did not see any snakes or poisonous insects inside the cave. The cave apparently had not been entered for many years. Obviously, it had not been discovered by soldiers of the Shore Command.

Once inside the cave, we could see the concrete structure from the light coming through the hole we made. The concrete entrance was four feet wide and six feet tall. At one time, there had been a door for the entrance. Now we could only see the huge steel hinges on the frame. The cave was about ten feet tall at the center and a semicircle of concrete formed the ceiling and walls. It became darker as we moved deeper inside. As we cautiously walked toward the back, we needed both flashlights to see the path where the concrete floor was littered with all sorts of debris. We proceeded very carefully and slowly. Ru-Kao and I walked side by side and the other two followed close behind. We carefully moved on each step, avoiding obstacles and unknown objects on the floor. Although this was in the hottest days of summer, deep inside the cave was cool, humid, dark, and ghostly quiet. When we talked, the echo of our voices sounded spooky. Tsang-Mou and Yu-Si were more scared of ghosts than Ru-Kao and me, but they tried hard to conceal their fears.

"Tien-Ren, are you sure there is no booby traps in the cave? You know those sneaky Japanese soldiers always did that to our soldiers during the war," Tsang-Mou said. I could detect from his voice he was shaking.

"Don't tell me you are scared. You are afraid of ghosts, aren't you?" I teased.

"No way. I am not afraid of any ghost," Tsang-Mou said. He sped up his pace, kicked a large object, and stumbled on the ground. He got up, dusted himself off, and said, "It's so dark here. I don't like it."

"All right, why don't you go outside and wait for us?" I said.

"I will just stay here. You guys go ahead," Tsang-Mou said. He stood still.

"If you see any ghosts, just give me a holler. I will come save you," Ru-Kao said, and he let out a loud laugh. We continued to move cautiously forward. Tsang-Mou quietly followed anyway.

The cave looked about fifty feet deep from our estimation, but it could be deeper. Near the back end of the cave, we saw several big piles of something stacked three feet high, and one big pile was at least five feet high.

"Look. I knew there are things hidden here. Let's take a close look!" Tsan-Mou shouted as he lunged toward the pile closest to him.

Ru-Kao pointed the flashlight at one of the piles. It consisted of complete cases, sealed and opened boxes, and loose small arms ammunition in an area of twenty square feet. Another pile next to it was comprised of the remainder of a weapons container. It appeared to have been damaged by a delayed explosive hastily set off by Japanese soldiers retreating toward the end of war. The explosion did some damage and littered the weapons throughout the cave, but it did not cause destruction. Most of the rifles were still intact. Upon closer examination, we found all the model 99 rifles had their bolts removed but otherwise were complete. In a bigger pile, deeper in the cave, were cases and loose cannon shells of the seventy-five-millimeter and some odd-caliber shells. Some of them were dented on the casing. A few light machineguns, also with missing bolt carriers, were piled in the back. The retreating Japanese apparently had tried to destroy all the caves when they surrendered. However, they were supposed to surrender the materials to the Chinese army. In any event, it was a real mess inside there for the military but a great fortune for us kids.

"From the way things are, I guessed the Japanese had stored these small arms and ammunition here for soldiers to defend from invaders to land on this beach," Yu-Si said.

"That sounds reasonable. This beach sure is an ideal place to land troops," Ru-Kao echoed.

"Let's take some of the rifles out and use them for training our boys. What do you think?" I asked.

"Good idea, but how many do you think we need to take?" Ru-Kao asked me.

"Let's see. We will give one to each of our buddies twelve years and older. There are enough rifles here for a company. How is that?" I said.

"I don't think the twelve-year-olds are strong enough to carry the rifle. I would just take eight of them for now," Tsan-Mou said.

"All right let's bring them out of the cave first," I said.

The four of us each carried two rifles out to the open first. Under the sunlight, I could see the guns were totally rusted.

"Let's go in to get some rifle ammunition," I said.

"What in the world do you want the ammunition for? You know the guns and the ammunition are dangerous combinations," Ru-Kao said.

"Well, I am familiar with the ammunition. Besides, the guns are not working. They are not dangerous if you know how to handle them. I plan to take the gunpowder out and use them for fireworks," I told the group. They did not disagree, so we went back in the cave again to haul out two sacks full of rifle bullets. It took us two trips to haul the rifles and rifle bullets to the edge of the mountainside, where we found an abandoned wooden shack near the compound, an ideal place to store everything.

After we returned home, we cleaned up and then gathered under that giant banyan tree again to brainstorm about what to do with the hoard.

"We could clean up the rusty rifles and play military drills," Yu-Si said.

"Sure, I believe the other kids would like to drill with the real rifles," Tsang-Mou said.

"All right, Tsang-Mou. How about you take charge of the training program and organize a platoon of soldiers?" I asked.

"Sure, I will do that. What about the rifle bullets?" Tsan-Mou asked.

"Of course, we will not issue any bullets for training," Ru-Kao said.

"I have some ideas to use the gunpowder for all sorts of fun things on the beach! I will tell you the details later, but first we need to get the gunpowder out from the bullets. Any volunteers?" I asked.

The three of them all raised their arms.

"The firing cap at the rear center, can you see this?" I took a bullet and pointed to the round cap at the end of the casing. "Don't ever hit it with any object. It may explode. Now we need to remove the bullet from the casing. Just put the bullet in a crack of a rock and bend it left and then right once. The bullet can be easily pulled out." I demonstrated the procedure right on a piece of large rock near me.

"Where can we find containers for the gunpowder?" Ru-Kao asked.

"Any dry empty canister will do," I said.

"I know where I can find some. I will be right back," Yu-Si said.

"All right let's go get a load of the ammunition and we will work right here," I said without thinking.

"Oh! No, we don't do it here. If someone sees the ammunition, we might be in big trouble," Ru-Kao said.

"You are right. Why don't we all meet at the big rock on the beach? Ru-Kao, you and I go fetch the ammo, and Tsan-Mou, you wait here for Yu-Si and bring him to the beach with the canisters," I announced.

On the beach, behind the big rock, no one could see us from the shore. We worked for about one hour to extract the gunpowder from the ammo of over 150 rifle rounds. We put them into two pint-size jars.

"We'd better hide this on the beach somewhere," Yu-Si said.

"How about right in the cavities on the rock? And it is high enough, so the waves will not hit the jars?" I suggested. All three kids agreed.

"Ru-Kao, I think we'd better report this to the officers in charge of this area. There might be many caves like the one we just found," I said.

"I agree. Let's go report this to Captain Yu's office," Rue-Kao suggested.

"Let's go now," Tsang-Mou urged.

We went to the captain's office near the entrance of the tunnel. In the small office, a sergeant was on duty.

"Good afternoon, Sergeant," We said.

"What do you kids want?" He was reading a newspaper. Impatiently, he raised his eyes at us and seemed annoyed.

"We want to report a destroyed ammunition dump in a cave near here," I said.

"So, what? There are hundreds of them like that in the mountains," he said impatiently.

"But they are dangerous! We found rifles and machineguns too," Ru-Kao said.

"You boys just stay away from those caves. You hear me? It is good you know they are dangerous. Go home," he said, and he immediately returned to read his newspaper.

At fifteen, we thought we knew everything there was to know under the sun. We did not argue with the officer, but we simply disregarded his advice entirely. We went back to the cave a few more trips in the following days and took more ammunition and broken pieces of weapons.

I showed other kids how to take a rifle shell apart safely and collected more gunpowder in several large metal cans. The casings with the primer caps intact were the dangerous part. We returned them to the cave. One day, I gathered a few kids and took a can of gunpowder to the beach, placed some in a sand hole, and then ignited it with a long-handled incense stick. The smoke and fire swooshed from the sand hole like a volcano. It attracted many spectators. Everybody in the group was excited by such an impressive display of fireworks. We took turns to ignite the gunpowder until all the gunpowder in that big metal can was gone. The four of us went back to the cave and gathered more sacks of rifle ammunition. The exact location of the cave was kept a secret from all other kids. We worked diligently to get more cans of gunpowder for future use.

The basic firework was soon becoming boring.

"We needed something more exciting. It must be replaced by a more elaborated display," Yu-Si told me a couple of days after our first fireworks on the beach.

"What do you have in mind?" I asked.

"Well, how about a cannon or mortar to shoot out the flames?" said Yu-Si.

"All right, I know just what we can do. Let's find a piece of large pipe and make mortar out it," I suggested.

"That sounds neat. You are the expert on weapons. How about make one and let's have some fun?" Ru-Kao urged me.

I found a piece of two-inch-diameter steel pipe left over by the water supply system construction and cut it into a two-foot-long piece with a hacksaw. I plugged a spent cannon shell casing to one end of the pipe. Then, a small opening was cut at the rear end of the casing for fuse insertion. Ru-Kao fixed a bipod made of two pieces of wood stick to complete the mortar. We had the mortar set up on the sandy beach about eighty yards from the compound and thirty yards from the water. When ready to fire, a piece of firecracker fuse was inserted into the small hole first. Gunpowder was then poured from the open end of the pipe.

"Now fellows, stand back. I am going to ignite the mortar!" I yelled. All bystanders stepped back at least twenty feet from where the mortar was. I bent down and ignited the fuse with an incense stick. A loud swooshing noise, flame, and smoke would shoot over tens of yards. It was just spectacular.

"Wow!" The crowd exploded in cheers. The four of us took turns to ignite the mortar until the gunpowder we brought with us was exhausted.

The next day, we returned to the beach with more gunpowder and the mortar.

"I think it will be more impressive if we put some sand in the tube. Let me try it first," I said. The other three were a bit gun-shy that day, so I did the show all by myself.

That day, about fifteen kids stood twenty feet behind the "mortar" in a semicircle, and the first round went off beautifully. The sand put in front of the gunpowder was sent high into the air with a puff of smoke and a loud whoosh. Everybody was excited and cheering when the "mortar" went off each time. In order to add to the excitement, I added a little bit more sand each time. The result was even more spectacular with more sand. It added loudness, smoke, and the distance of the flame. So, I added more and more sand on top of the gunpowder each time. Then, this time, just as I bent down to ignite the fuse, there was such a loud explosion. My ear was deafened and ringing for a few minutes.

After I collected myself, I found I was not hurt. I touched my head, my arms, and my legs. They were there without any pain.

I looked around and found no one in the audience was hurt either. However, the mortar was not there anymore—not even a fractured piece. We looked for a long time in a five-hundred-yard radius in the mountainside and on the beach, but it was never found. I was really scared when I thought what damage it might have done to the spectators and myself. With such a powerful explosion, we were so lucky that no one was killed that day. Some houses in the compound had their windows facing the beach shatter into pieces.

Many people in the compound and soldiers came to investigate what had happened. I admitted to the officer in charge that I had caused the explosion. Some people went to get Mama and told her about the near disaster. Mama came out took me by the ear into the house.

"I know you are curious and venturous, but this is pure stupidity," Mama scolded me. I had never seen her so angry in the past. "You could get yourself killed and take some innocent people with you. Do you know that?"

"I am sorry, Mama. I was stupid. I will never play with the ammunition again," I promised.

"You are grounded for two weeks," Mama told me. This was the first time Mama handed me such serious punishment.

Baba found out the situation, but he was not as upset with me. He ordered the soldiers to seal off the caves in the nearby mountains. We had to pay for the damages to our neighbors' windows. Although I was not punished enough to fit my dumb deeds, I did learn a big lesson. Luckily none of the kids were prohibited to play with me after the two-week grounding. I just had to control myself not to venture into things that I really did know enough about.

CHAPTER 4

THE TURNING POINT

Although the provincial high school was the elite school in southern Taiwan, my one semester study in the Trinity College had prepared me much farther than the demand from the current school. Therefore, it was easy for me to get good scores in the entrance examinations. My grades in the final semester of ninth grade were quite good and I graduated from the junior high in December 1949. There was an entrance examination to enter the senior high—the tenth grade. I took the test, did well, and was accepted to the freshman class starting in January 1950. Many of my classmates in the ninth grade did not make the entrance examination to the same school they had graduated from. It was a very tough school.

But because of the easy success in the junior high school, I started the senior high on the wrong foot as soon as the school started. I was involved with some classmates I had befriended the first day I entered the school. Hsin-Yen Wu and Tsi-Yuan Tsao both were six feet, three inches tall, quite muscular, and athletic. They were new members of a small gang organized in the school by sophomores and seniors. The two quickly became the chiefs of the small gangsters' group. I had observed them dressed in the sailor-blue shirts, cowboy jeans, and cowboy boots. The stylish thing for the gang members was to wear an undershirt and throw the blue shirt on their shoulders, walking in warbling goose steps and looking down upon everyone else on the campus. The school had a hair code that was easier to shave the head clean, but the gangsters would wear crew cuts. Because the two chiefs were my good friends from the junior high, I thought it was cool to go along with them when Hsin-Yen asked me to join them. I was accepted by other gang members because of the big muscles on my arms and shoulders, and it might make the gangs look better to have a strong muscleman around them.

The gang members spent a lot of time making trouble for "weak" students and even making fun with some teachers. We would hang around at the campus building corners, teasing passersby or making fun of certain people we disliked. There was a classmate of mine, Sho-Chun Liu, who was very slim, with fair skin, and he walked like a girl. We called him Miss Liu and teased him endlessly. Sho-Chun was very patient with the gang members and never responded. I often joined in with other gang members to make cruel remarks to him, but he never protested either. One day we were alone near the library. Sho-Chun pulled me to the side and asked me, "Why do you want to hang around with the gangsters? I hate them." Tears flowed down his cheeks. All along, I thought he never minded all the cruel teases.

"I am sorry. I didn't know that hurts you. I thought we were just having fun. I will not do it to you again," I said, and I felt rotten inside. I never teased Sho-Chun again, but I could not stop the other guys from the continued cruelty. When I told Hsin-Yen, he said he couldn't stop the other guys either because that would make him look weak as a gang leader who was supposed to be the tough and heartless type.

All the gang members like me were about sixteen to eighteen years old. When we roamed the campus like a band of conquerors, we felt as if we were on top of the world. We thought we were more superior to those who were afraid of us. As far as I knew, the gangs never did anything bad, such as beating people up or stealing. I participated with the gang activities inside the school only. Outside of school, I did not go with them because police were everywhere, as the martial law was enforced; the gangs' activities were subdued outside of the campus. Nevertheless, I thought it was fun to hang around with these cool and tough guys.

Rue-Kao was enrolled in the City High School which was in the mid-way to the provincial high School I attended. We often rode bike to school together and said good-by in the front gate of the City High. At the age of 16 he was a superb sportsman and good student in his class of about 36 people. Among the 36 students, two brothers, apparently an identical twin also named Chang the same last name as Rue-Kao. The twins were also 16 years old, but they were very different types. They were big and tall and weighed above 200 pounds each. They often bullied other students to submission and laughed loudly.

For some reasons unknown to me they would pick on Rue-Kao for no apparent provocation. This was going on for a while. One day, the twin stopped Rue-Kao on his way out of school.

"Hay! You chicken shit. Where do you think you are going?" One of the twins barked.

"I am going home. Is there anything wrong?" Answered Rue-Kao.

"I don't like you. You better not show up at the school tomorrow or you will regret it." Said another one of the twins.

"I am not afraid you! Just do whatever you want to do." Rue-Kao barked back.

"OK. Then we will see you here. You chicken shit!" The first twin barked.

When Rue-Kao saw me that evening he told me about the twin's threat. Rue-Kao knew my participation in the gangs' activities, so he was hoping I could help him out. I recalled my own experience of being bullied. How the group of gangsters bullied me, how I sought the help from the one friend his father owned a tofu shop and how they came to my aid at the school entrance.

"OK. Rue-Kao just go to school as usual tomorrow and I will see to it that that will not bother you again," said I confidently.

"That will be a good thing. But are you sure you can get help from your gangs?" Rue-Kao was not sure of anything.

"I will arrange a meeting with them, and I am sure they will help out. Just don't worry."

The next morning, I told the incident to Hsin-Yen, the leader of the gang. He knew Rue-Kao from my introduction, and he was totally understanding of the situation.

"Don't worry I will get a few of the members to go with us this afternoon. You just be there at five o'clock," he said.

Then he walked away to gather the members. An hour later he had gotten eight members of the gang together. He briefed them about what happened.

"We will go our separate ways and then meet at the right side of the City High's gate. This way we will not draw attention to anyone," Xin-Yen told the group.

In the afternoon about four thirty, we took our bike and rode separately toward the City High. In about twenty minutes all members had arrived the place. We found a spot about twenty-five feet from the entrance of the school and waited. As we watched the people coming and going out the school the twin showed up first. They did not notice our presence. When Rue-Kao came out of the school the twin immediately stopped him.

"We told you not to come to the school. And you did," They started to push Rue-Kao.

Just at that moment, I yelled loud, "Stop. You fat guys."

And the gang members swarmed the twins. They were shocked by the presence of so many gangs and froze up.

"If I see you bother my friend again, your head will say goodbye to your shoulders. Do you hear me?" I yelled as loud as I could.

The twins just ran away as fast as they could and never bother Rue-Kao again.

Our Chinese literature teacher was a middle-aged man with unusually white skin, so we called him the "white monkey." He was a good and tough teacher, but he also liked to discipline students based on his own feelings. One day he stopped me in the hallway. "Why do you have to walk like a gorilla, or you think you are a Superman?" he told me.

"Mr. Tseng, I don't understand what you mean. Can you tell me why?" I was truly puzzled because I had never done anything to provoke him, I thought.

"Well, then why do you walk with your shoulder lifted up so high?" he asked with an expression of disgusting.

"Mr. Tseng, I am not doing that. It is just my muscle that makes me looked that way," I explained. He reached over with his right hand, feeling out my left shoulder.

"Oh, you have grown too much muscle. I wish you would have grown a bit more of your brain. You are not doing well in my class, you know," he said, and he just walked away.

That was a minor problem for me in the first few months in senior high school. One afternoon we were waiting for the teacher of the geography class to show up. He was about five minutes late. As he walked near the classroom entrance, every Taiwanese student was yelling, "Ilasaii! Ilasaii!" I could not understand the meaning of the Japanese word, but I also yelled, "Ilasaii!" as he walked in the room mad. He immediately turned around and reported this to the dean of academic affairs. It turned out *ilasaii* means "heron" in Japanese. He had long legs and walked with a kick in each step.

Ten minutes later, the dean of academic affairs, Mr. Chang, came to the classroom. "You have behaved badly. So, I will give you all a failing grade in this class unless you tell me who yelled."

No one responded to him.

"All right, I will make a deal with you. Anyone who admits to the yelling will not be punished, and I will let all of you go free."

I thought that was good deal. "I did," I responded as I raised my right hand.

"The rest of you are dismissed. You come with me." He looked at me. I hoped he did not trick me into that.

I followed him to his big office. He went to sit in his chair and let me stand there in front of his desk.

"Normally, I would expel you, but because you did really well in you entrance examinations, I will just give you a suspended expulsion if you behave yourself from today on," he said while looking at those papers on his desk. I had never liked this man who had a nickname of Dog Head Chang.

"Mr. Chang, I hope you are not serious about this. I raised my hand because you said you will not punish me and let the whole class go free. I think you have tricked me, and I don't think this is right. Besides, the whole class was yelling the same word," I said angrily.

"I don't care what you think. I must punish someone. You are dismissed."

I turned around and angrily walked out of his office. Before school ended that day, the notice of my punishment was posted on the school bulletin board. On the way home, I was so upset that I daydreamed all sorts of revenge acts against that Dog Head. He was such a dishonest guy and should not have been overseen a school. He must be punished for his deed. I could ask the gangs to beat him up on his way home. They would beat him up so badly that he would look for help from me then I would let him go. I could also shoot him with my slingshot and make him to suffer the pain. But then what good could it do to me? I was already punished and announced to the entire school. Nothing I did would alter the damage to me.

Depressed, I turned to Baba when he set his foot in the house. "Baba, the Dog Head Chang has cheated me into admitting a bad deed that was committed by the whole class," I blurted out. "He then gave me a suspended expulsion. I think it is unfair."

"Slow down and tell me what has happened to you," Baba said as he always did when things turned red hot; he would be very cool. I told him the whole story as it was.

"All right, son, you come with me to the school right this minute," he said, and then he called the office to get his Jeep ready. We needed to get there before the school officials went home that day. The Jeep took us to the school in fifteen minutes. Baba walked straight toward the principal's office and announced he wanted to see the principal. Mr. Wang, a very respectable man in his late thirties, was the principal. He came and greeted us into his office. Baba made me to stay and listen to what he had to say.

"Colonel Cheng, what can I do for you today?" Mr. Wang asked.

"Mr. Wang, you are a well-respected educator. I am very pleased to have this opportunity to talk to you today. I think you can do something for a student and the school at the same time," Baba said. I knew he was disarming the principal.

"Well, if there is anything, I can do to help my student, I am always happy to do it unless it is a matter of competency or grades," he said.

"That is very good of you. I am sure you will agree with me that we need to teach our next generation to be honest. To do so, we the teacher and parents must show them by our deeds. Do you agree with me?" Baba asked.

"Absolutely, we want to be the example as educators, and honesty is the foremost of all characters we want our next generation to have." Mr. Wang echoed Baba's point.

"Of course, trickery is a form of dishonesty in my view. Do you agree with me?"

"Certainly, I think trickery is a worse form of dishonesty, because it would hurt people. Now what seems to be the problem, Colonel Cheng?" he asked.

"I have been teaching myself, so I understand how important it is to punish people for wrongdoings. The purpose is to guide them to the right path and not to hurt them. An educator is like Jesus who would sacrifice himself to guide the lost lambs and not to beat and hurt the lamb who wandered into a wrong path. Furthermore, if the student really did no wrong but was trying to bail out the class, would you punish the student?"

"I see your point," he said to Baba. Then he turned toward me and asked, "Please tell me what has happened."

I told him the story exactly as it had happened.

"Mr. Wang, I did not know what that word meant, and I did not know it was the nickname of the teacher. Besides, I was yelling only once following the whole class," I reported. "When Mr. Chang told us to have one admission then he would forgive the whole class, I thought it was good for the whole class and I was not to be punished."

"I see. Please give me moment. I will see Mr. Chang in his office and come right back." He then called his secretary to serve another mug of hot tea to Baba.

Ten minutes later, he emerged from the connecting door to the dean's office and went to Baba. His face was red, and it appeared that he had been upset with someone else.

"It is a mistake we have made. I apologize to you and your son. The suspended expulsion announcement will be corrected right away." He then shook Baba's hand before we left his office. On the way home, I admired Baba totally for his ability to convince the principal. I also felt grateful and appreciated his total trust in me.

The next day an announcement was made on the bulletin board that I was exonerated of any wrongdoing and thus no punishment was to be on my record. Mr. Chang would turn his head away from me whenever we bumped into each other on the campus. It turned out that teacher we teased was Mr. Chang's wife's cousin. When the story was told on campus, people who had a low opinion of Mr. Chang now had proof on their hunch. Now his nickname became "Dirty Dog Head," because his family name Chang sounded like "dirty" in Mandarin.

Getting out of trouble from teachers was one thing, but my poor schoolwork was totally another matter. Mr. Tseng was right when he commented that I should have developed more in my brain instead of my muscles. As the time wore on, my schoolwork was completely neglected that semester between basketball games, soccer games, daily ball practices, my electronics hobbies, and most of all, the large amount of time spent hanging with the gang members. I missed some term papers and did poorly in monthly examinations. Strangely it did not bother me or alarm me a bit. The gang members lived in a totally different world from other students. They had their own priority of life. At that moment in time, it was more important to gain the approval of fellow gang members than anything else in school. While I was immersed in the gang activities, I was not aware of the real impact to my life. It was cool and fun to hang around these characters, but deep in my mind, I knew it was not right to waste my time like that. However, I was not able to come to terms with the reality and I did not have any reason just to quit the gang. A semester went by quickly before I knew it.

When the report card came, I was shocked to see I was ranked number 40 out of a class of forty-two students. The other two guys at the bottom were flunked out and I barely made the passing grade. In the past, I was never a good student, but I was able to maintain in the middle of class ranks. This report card was certainly an embarrassing blow to me. I could not hide the fact and had to go face Mama and Baba with the bad report. I knew it would not be pleasant. I could see Baba get very upset and yell at me, and Mama might cry when she saw this poor showing of her son she had always trusted. When I went home that late evening, Mama was cooking in the kitchen and Baba was reading newspapers in the living room. I showed the report card to Mama first. She put her chopping knife down and took the card and read it again in disbelief.

"Ren, it is very bad. Isn't it?" Mama said. "You'd better show it to Baba now."

"Yes. Mama, I am sorry."

I went to the living room and timidly handed the report card to Baba. Baba looked it over, raised his sharp eyes at me in a disgusted expression, and my heart sunk to the bottom of the ocean floor. He got up from the couch and waved me to go to the side of the window. I guessed he just wanted to cool off his anger a little before talking to me.

"Son, in the Cheng family," he said in a surprisingly calm voice, "we were not rich or famous, but from your great grandfather and your grandfather to me, we were all very good students and did well in school. As a matter of fact, we were all number 1 in our classes. I don't know if you are going to be the one to break the family tradition. However, I trust that if you want to do it well, you sure can be the number 1 student in your class. Am I right?"

"I am very sorry about the bad grades, Baba. I will study harder and do my best next semester."

Mama now walked into the living room to join us. "I know you can do better, if you just spend a little more time in your schoolwork," Mama said.

"Yes, Mama, I promise I will do my best. You and Baba will not see a bad report card again," I promised. I felt so ashamed and wanted to cry, but I toughed it out.

I decided to do something about this and show Mama and Baba that I could make it to the top if I tried, and I had to try. I wanted to do it without sacrificing my sports and my electronic hobbies. However, I knew I had to break up with the few buddies in the gang. I understood the risk of breaking up with the gangsters once I was initiated, but I had no choice now. One thing working in my favor was the leader of the gang, Hsin-Yen, was my good friend. So, I found an opportunity when Hsin-Yen was together with the gang one day.

"Look, fellows. I am in deep trouble with my father because I was almost flunked out from my class. If I don't bring back a better report card next semester, I don't know what my father will do to me. I need to study seriously from now on. So, if you guys will forgive me, I will not be with you in any of the future activities," I told them. I was more than a little scared because we had sworn that we would not quit the gang under any circumstances. I had heard other people breaking their vow got hurt badly when they decided to leave the gang.

"Well, you know the penalty for quitting the organization?" Je-Sho Niu, a seventeen-year-old tough guy, said to me menacingly.

"I really have to spend time to study or my dad will kill me," I exaggerated.

"We have no use of such a bookworm anyway. Let him go!" Hsin-Yen told the others. Then he turned his head to me and told me, "Go ahead. Do your own thing and get out of here." He waved his long arm for me to leave. I knew he was trying to help me out. The rest of them just laughed at me and teased me a little as I walked away from them, but they left me alone from that day on. I knew if it was not for Hsin-Yen, I might have to take some beating or at least some rough insults from other gang members. After I left the gang, I felt such a relief and wondered why I had joined them in the first place!

At home, I drafted up a plan for my schoolwork that evening and decided to drop some of my sporting activities, such as volleyball, track, and swimming. I determined to devote my effort to study very seriously. At the same time, I remain active on the soccer team and the basketball team. I also kept the volunteer work as the equipment repairman for the physics laboratory. Of course, my radio/electronics hobbies had to be continued.

My studying plan was very simple. The most crucial strategy was to know my study each day instead of waiting until the day before examination. I decided to complete each day's assignment right at school and then stop by the elementary school, just outside the housing compound on my way home, to review for one hour what I had learned in classes that day. After that, I would practice basketball for one or two hours with my buddies in the compound before going home for supper. I did not tell any friends in my class or in the compound about my new study plans since I only changed my extracurricular activities very slightly. No one even noticed the changes of my activities at school or at home.

That plan worked well for me. In classes I paid attention to my teachers and turned in my assignments on time. That was a big turnaround for me that startled many of the teachers, because I was tardy in turning in assignments and my works were lousy in the first semester. The Chinese literature teacher, Mr. Chen, an older man in his forties, had great suspicion in my sudden improvement and thought I had someone do my homework for me. One day, he stopped me cold on the track to the basketball court after lunch break.

"Your homework is so much better than you did last semester. Did you have someone else do it for you? Hum!" he asked with his usual arrogant way, tilting his head with a sneaky smile on his face.

"No, Mr. Chen, I do my homework myself. No one is helping me," I replied.

"Well, then come in my office and write a short paper for me using the classical Chinese," he demanded.

"Sure, Mr. Chen. You want me to do it right now? I have a basketball prep session for tonight's game."

"Well, this is more important. Follow me to my office," he ordered.

I followed him to his office. He pointed for me to sit on a side table.

"I want you to read this article and write a one-page critique using classical Chinese," he said. "How much time do you need to do it? Is one hour enough for you?"

I looked at the article and said, "I will do it in half an hour."

It was something I used to do for Baba when I was in Fu-shin-gon years ago. To me, it was just a piece of cake. Anyway, I finished the writing within the time limit. Apparently satisfied, he said, "The writing is not that great, but I think you are all right." That was the highest praise he would give to anybody in my class. From that day on, he stopped looking at me as if I had stolen something from him.

The three or four top students in the class had always banded together, acting like an elite gang and looking down upon the lower ranked classmates, especially the ones at the bottom of the class—like me. In the past, I was too busy playing balls and going with the gangsters in the first semester, so I did not notice their arrogant attitudes. Now that I was more serious about studies, I could feel the hurt with the way they looked at me and the way they talked to me. A month or so into the semester, they were surprised to see my test scores were better than theirs, as teachers always announced the scores in the class. The few top students in my class felt very uneasy and thought I had scored well by sheer luck or cheating in the first few tests. The number 1 student in my class, Chi-Cho Hsia, a stocky, short fellow and a self-appointed genius, who'd never laid his eyes on me before, pulled me on the side one day after the advanced algebra class.

"I don't believe you beat me twice in a row in the last two tests. I know you barely passed the minimum score without being flunked out last semester," Chi-Cho told me, looking straight in my eyes. "And are you quitting being involved with those ball games, or now you have a tutor at home? I am just curious." He sure was arrogant, but since he had never talked to me before this day, I even felt honored to have this top guy talking to me in such length even though he was not at all friendly.

"Well, tell you the truth, I have spent at least one hour per day after school and review everything I learned that day before playing ball," I told him the truth.

"Is that all you do differently from last semester?" He was not convinced at all and thought I was lying to him.

"Of course, I am also paying much more attention in classes too," I said, but I didn't say I was aiming at his title, as I already sensed the threat he felt.

"Hum! I wish you luck," he said with a hint that I would never make it.

That just made my determination to beat him ever stronger. After that day, I kept my study plan as I had drafted without being affected by his intimidation. When my test scores persisted through the first two monthly examinations, the top three guys knew they were seriously challenged. None of the top bookworms participated in any sport activities while I played on both basketball and soccer teams. The other three top guys gradually came to me as if they had given me a promotion or did me a favor, but I never hung around with them and kept my buddies in the sporting and the radio/electronics groups.

When the end of the semester result was announced, I did achieve my goal and fulfilled the promise I made to Mama and Baba, and that was the first time ever I had the taste of being number 1 in classes. The feeling was good and sweet, but I vowed that I would never act like the other top-ranked students after I had been treated by them being at the bottom once. The only classes I did not get the top grade in were civics and music, but they did not affect my average. When I presented my report card at the end of the semester to Mama and Baba, they were very pleased but not surprised.

"I know you can do it. I am so proud of you," Mama beamed.

"That is our family tradition to do well with schoolwork. I am very happy too. Now you need to keep up with it and don't slip from the top," Baba said.

To my classmates and teachers, the dramatic change in my class standing made some big waves among them for a while; the top-ranked students felt very hurt from being beaten by a bottom-ranked fellow student. On the surface, they acted cordially, but I knew they were not happy to drop from their old ranks. My old buddies were very happy for me, and that was very important to me. Our master teacher of the class, Mr. Tsang, collected the class on the last day in school and gave us a lecture.

"I want you fellows to see the example Tien-Ren Cheng has made. He was at the bottom of the class last semester, but when he pays attention to studies, he has transformed into the number 1 student in the class. I don't think he is smarter than any of you people, but he has applied himself. If he can do it, there is no reason why you can't do the same," Mr. Tsang said. That pep talk was not very complimentary to me. I was wondering why he would talk to the entire class of students like that, but I soon realized that Mr. Tsang's performance was determined by how well his class of students would do in passing college entrance exams after we had graduated from the high school.

To me, now the tough challenge became apparent; it was easier to reach the top in a class for the first time, but to stay on top of the class for the rest of the high school years would be a very tough thing. There were four more semesters to go. Like everything else, the title was always a goal for challengers. I really had not sacrificed a great deal of fun and had not become a real bookworm. I knew I was not smarter than most of my classmates and was afraid if others just came up with a study plan like mine, I would be knocked off the top rank in the class. I had done my best and couldn't imagine sacrificing much more of my other activities. I would not drop any of my current sport activities. Certainly, I would not stop my electronics hobby, even for the sake of better grades.

CHAPTER 5

GOOD-BYE, LION

It was like a fixed routine for Lion. Each morning from Monday to Saturday, Lion would walk me from my house to the gate of the compound, and then sat there until I entered the dark tunnel. He somehow knew what time I would come home from school and never failed to greet me enthusiastically right at the gate. When I did my homework after school, studying in the elementary school, Lion did not know I was just a few hundred feet from the gate; he would just sit at the side of the gate and patiently waited. When I played basketball after my studying session, he would be waiting a few yards from the basketball court, lying on the grass and watching intensely. The basketball court was right outside the gate to the compound. In Taiwan, there was no shortage of food, so we fed Lion with a mixture of rice and leftover dishes from the day. Lion had no need to hunt for food like my other dogs in rural Chunking. As a matter of fact, Lion had never had the need to hunt since he came to our home—from Nanjing to Shanghai then Fu-chow and now in Kao-Shiung, Taiwan. He was a well-fed and chubby, overgrown three-year-old puppy.

Ever since we landed in Taiwan, we never used the leash on Lion. He roamed freely in the compound and occasionally went with his dog friends to play in areas near the shore. At home, he slept on a pad in the hallway between my room and the living room. When any stranger came to the door, he would make a winding sound to alert us. If we did not respond for a minute, then he would bark loudly. When the family members were around, Lion would let people pet him; otherwise, he would run away from people or show his teeth to people he didn't like.

When President Chiang Kai-Sheik came south to stay in the beach white house, the security people would come to my house to take Lion to a temporary shelter far from the president's house so that the old man would not be disturbed by the barking dog. It was hard for me to see those guys treating Lion so roughly. Lion would cry and struggle while being hauled into a cage. The security people would not even tell me where they sent Lion to stay. Normally in two or three days they would bring Lion back to us. Lion would greet everyone of the family enthusiastically, hopping and whining for minutes.

Lion was a one-man dog, and he would not go with any of my friends even when cookies were offered to him. Mama told me when I left for school, Lion would sleep or follow her around in the house until late afternoon just before I came home. Baba also loved Lion very much, and Lion knew it. He often lay next to Baba's sofa when he was drinking tea and smoking his cigarettes. Another of Lion's good friends was Wye-Gong, who would give Lion a few scraps of biscuits whenever Lion went to his room. When Wye Gong went to the beach for a dip, he would take Lion with him, but Lion would just sit there watching and never went to go into the water. As far as I was concerned, we had five family members living in the house. Lion was truly an integral part of the family. When I played with my friends in the compound, Lion would be on my side all the time. If Lion thought someone was attacking me, he would come to my rescue by hanging on to another kid's trousers. I was truly blessed with such a smart and loyal companion.

One day, when I came home from studies at the elementary school, Lion was not at the gate. I went back to the gate and called him around that area. There was no sight of Lion. I went home and asked Mama about Lion. She said she had not seen Lion for quite a while. That was not normal for Lion. Worried, I asked Mama to help me look for him. Mama and I searched the whole compound and the vicinities but there was no trace of Lion. I kept looking for him until late in the night. Depressed and worried, I knew Lion would not wander away from the house and get lost, something was terribly wrong. My dog in rural Chunking was caught by a butcher and killed for meat, but that was during the war. People were hungry and desperate then. Now catching other people's dog for meat was illegal. Besides, we live in the secured area; no dogcatchers could ever come close to the tunnel. Baba heard about Lion missing and called the security officer to look out for Lion. No one could provide any clue that night. I went to bed after midnight, hoping Lion would show up, but he didn't. I had a terrible night with all sorts of unpleasant dreams.

The next day, I got up very early in the morning, and as I opened the door, my heart sunk to the floor. Poor Lion was lying on the ground with his guts hung out of his belly.

"Mama, Baba, quick! Lion is hurt very badly!" I cried to my parents.

Both Baba and Mama rushed to the back door in pajamas. Mama saw how bad it was and cried. Baba immediately telephoned the veterinarian at home to wake him up. The veterinarian lived not far from the compound and came within ten minutes with his medical kit to rescue Lion.

"It is very bad, because the wound is at least ten hours old. The dog has bled a lot in the last few hours, so you don't even see any blood on the floor," the veterinarian said.

"Please help Lion. He came all the way from Nanjing. I don't want to lose him. Please save him," I begged.

"I will try, but you know I am not god," he said.

The tone sent a chill through my spine and I was frightened. Lion was lying on his right side. The wound was on his belly toward the left side. A blob of guts was outside of the two-inch gaping hole. His underbelly had dried blood, but his upper coat was clean. When I called his name, he opened his eyes only slightly and tried to raise his head. The vet crouched on the ground and examined Lion visually.

"Would you hold him down and let me clean up his intestines before I stich him up?" the vet asked me.

I held Lion's front feet and Baba held his rear feet for the vet. Lion was still motionless at that point. The vet then carefully cleaned the guts that were out of the belly with rubbing alcohol and a swath.

"It looks like a knife wound. I am not optimistic the dog will live," he said as he worked.

At one point when the vet finished cleaning and pushed the guts back into his belly, Lion was obviously in great pain. During the confusion, while I was holding his legs, he bit me at my palm and punctured two holes on my hand, so blood dripped out. The veterinarian gave Lion a shot of painkiller and carefully closed the wound with some surgical thread.

"Let him rest and see how it develops in the next twenty-four hours." The vet got up.

Mama could not look at Lion during the rescue operation and just stayed inside the house. I knew she was very upset too at that time.

I gently picked up Lion and brought him inside the house, where Mama had put extra padding on Lion's bed. I set him down carefully. Lion was breathing as usual with his eyes closed. I hoped the vet's work and the rest would help him recover.

We turned our attention to other matters, while we thought Lion was sleeping. Moments later when I went to check on him, he disappeared again. I immediately went out looking for him. He had just wandered into the mountain path near the compound, slowly and listlessly. I called him, but he did not even turn his head. I knew then Lion did not want to die in the house. I followed him about ten feet behind, and after another thirty feet on the path, he just stopped, lay down, and stopped breathing. I cried and picked him up in my arms. I brought him home for Mama to say good-bye to him. Mama held me and Lion's body together. We sobbed uncontrollably

The Island Heaven

for losing this loyal, longtime friend who had traveled so many miles and cities with us.

Mama found a towel. We wrapped Lion's body in it. Sadly, I found Lion's body so light. He had lost much of the weight after the fatal wound. I then took a spade and held the wrapped body in my arms to the far end of the mountainside, where I dug a small grave for Lion. I stood there in front of the mud pile for quite a while and left feeling so empty.

When Baba found out Lion was dead, he too had tears rolling down his cheeks. We felt very sad for quite a few days. A week later, a captain brought a young soldier to our house in the evening. Only Mama and I were home.

"We found this soldier caused your dog's death. I want him to tell you and see what you want to do with him," the captain said. And then he turned to the soldier. "Tell him what you have done."

"I am very sorry about hurting your dog. I was bitten by a dog when I was young, and I am still afraid of dogs. The other day I was standing guard in the area when I saw this dog running toward me. I was trying to scare the dog away with the rifle and bayonet, but he ran right by the tip of the bayonet. I didn't see any blood. I didn't even know I had punctured him until a day later. I am very sorry," he said. The young man was frightened.

"What has happened was a very unfortunate accident. Since you were not killing him intentionally, I can't fault you for that," Mama said. Then she told the captain, "We will not blame anybody for this accident."

"I am very, very sorry," said the soldier. He then came over put his arms on my shoulders. I was still in shock and could not say anything to him. The captain saluted Mama and quickly led the soldier back to the camp.

At school, in the Chinese composition class, I wrote a eulogy for Lion. After the paper was graded and returned to me, I took it to Lion's gravesite and burned the paper. He was not quite four years old.

CHAPTER 6

THE ROAD TO ADULTHOOD

At fifteen years old, I thought we had grown up to our prime age. It was a dreadful thought to be as old as twenty years old. The few kids, all age fourteen to sixteen, on the basketball team talked about our teammates one day.

"I feel so sorry for Lieutenant Ku. I think he is too old on the team, but I just can't tell him about it," said Kai Liang, our captain of the team.

"How old do you think he is?" Ru-Kao asked.

"Well, from the looks, I'd say he is over twenty-two years old," said Kai. "I guess we will give him some slacks on the court."

That was the way we thought about our ages. I was especially concerned that in just a few months I would be sixteen years old and then everything would go downhill! I tried to think how I could make every minute count during a day and enjoy every moment of it. But time did wait. No matter what I did, a day would go by quickly. Soon I was sixteen years old without any noticeable change in me. The age matter was then forgotten.

The Island Heaven

At home, I thought Mama and Baba were old and not current in what was going on in the world. I thought I knew everything there was to know in the world. That made Baba very unhappy and he told Mama that I was rebellious, but I wasn't. I was just trying to tell them I knew what I was doing with my life. Baba would patiently tell me historical events of ancient Chinese scholars, famous emperors, and generals. It was interesting to me, but when the speech turned into hours and covered dinnertime, I was frustrated. Of course, Baba did not take my impatience lightly. On top of the speech, he would lecture me on my attitude. As a result, I tried to avoid seeing him as much as I could. I would play basketball with the boys in the compound until way after suppertime, then I would go home to eat. Mama showed her understanding of the situation and did not give me any hard times.

My weightlifting, and other exercises had built up my muscle and strength to far above average in school. As a matter of fact, I was stronger than many of the fellows in track and field. Six months after I found the mini railroad wheels, I was able to lift them with only one hand while Yu-Si, now over six feet tall, could not even lift it off the ground with both hands. Other kids in the compound did not want to risk injuries by weightlifting exercises. I was quite alone in my exercise program but kept it up every day.

In school, arm-wrestling tournaments were in session year-round. I had never participated in the competition in my first year in high school, but I became more interested when I entered the sophomore class. The champion at that time was Chun-Shu Yeh, a tall and stout fellow of about 180 pounds who had no competition in arm wrestling for at least six months. I was only five feet, six, and weighed 130 pounds. When I signed up for the competition, I had to compete from the bottom echelon and move up. It took me a whole month to beat just about everyone in the tournament the first time around. I thought the numerous crab claws I ate years ago must have helped me to have such strength. I finally moved up the ranks to meet with this Hercules. He was very strong indeed, and his size was quite intimidating. I lost to him in all the rounds in the following three days, but I was not discouraged. Although he beat me, I could see it was not easy for him. So, I thought there had to be a way I could beat him.

I studied his tactics, his strengths, and his weakness. I had found out that he did not have any tactics at all, just brute force because he did not think he needed any. His strength was the raw power of his muscles and physical size. Since he had not been defeated by anyone in the school before, so he was careless and often lacked concentration. Proportional to my shorter arms, his longer arms sure gave me the advantage in leverage. My tactic was to give him surprises by sudden moves and using the leverage principles to beat him. That afternoon, in front of a group of judges and spectators, I first just held the position without pushing back. After two minutes, he lost a bit of concentration. I suddenly used all I had, and in a quick push, I put his arm down for the first time. Everybody applauded. Chun-Shu, instead of getting embarrassed, got up and shook my hand. I knew because he was a man of high confidence. From that point on, we beat each other back and forth. He did win more often than I did. No one else in this high school had such a close match with him as I did. The two of us were not beatable by others for more than two years until we graduated from the high school.

He became an air force pilot later and was the first ROC pilot to shoot down a MIG 17 fighter in a dogfight over the Taiwan Straits. Years later, he was promoted to a general in the Taiwan air force.

Time flew by so quickly that we had been away from the mainland for more than a year now. Mama was worried about Grandma Liu, but all the communications were cut off between Taiwan and the mainland by both governments. Anyone caught by the police sending or receiving letters to and from mainland would be treated as a spy for the Communists. No shortwave radios were allowed at

At the age of 17 in Kao-Shiung

home, and telephone calls to relatives on the mainland were out of question. All we knew about what was happening on the mainland was from the controlled government news and word of mouth from people who came from Hong Kong. After Fu-chow lost in mid-August, the entire Fujian Province was lost by early September 1949. However, the Nationalists still controlled much of Sichuan including Chunking. Government officials still working in Chunking had been evacuated by mid-September. In October that year, the entire mainland was taken by the Red Army. The People's Republic of China was inaugurated on October 1, 1949, in Beijing.

According to Taiwan newspaper accounts, mainlanders were suffering from oppression, starvation, and more. We felt very lucky that we got out of there just in time. We never knew what happened to Grandma Liu, Uncle I-Quay, and other relatives, and we were very worried. The government in Taiwan under President Chiang Kai-Sheik promised people that he would lead our troops to counterattack the mainland's illegal regime and regain control of the country. The presses printed about the counterattack, the radio talked about the counterattack, we sang songs about the counterattack, and after a while, we really believed it. Many mainlanders in Taiwan were preparing what to do when we finally returned to the mainland.

"I wonder how Wye Po is these days. The Communists are taking properties away from landlords and giving them to poor peasants. Since she was collecting rents to make a living, I hope they will not treat her like a landlord," Mama said me one day.

"Don't worry, Mama, the Communists have smart security people. They will know she does not have any money. They only prosecute the rich people. I think Granduncle and his family are in real trouble now." I was very worried. What was happening to the uncles and the aunt? I had heard and read a lot of horror stories that had happened to people who stayed behind on the mainland that rich people were tortured to death or humiliated in front the whole community. Sometimes we just dismissed the stories as the propaganda by the Nationalist government. I was content with the life in Taiwan and really had no great desire to return to the mainland at this time.

"Baba, when will we counterattack?" I asked him one day after dinner.

"I really don't know. It is a military secret currently. We want to surprise our enemy when the time comes," he told me.

I was happy it would not happen any time soon. I just had too much fun that I'd never experienced while I lived on the mainland.

In May 1950, the massive Red Army and its navy mounted a massive assault against the forward island of Kinmen and Machu. The news came on the radio that shocked the population and frightened people who just escaped from mainland. Troops in Taiwan were on full alert. The martial law was strictly enforced. After the news broke out, Baba stayed in his headquarters day and night and did not come home for meals while the situation was very tense. He had to be prepared for the attack by the Communists.

"If they take Kinmen and Machu, the next move will be Taiwan," Mama said, apparently very worried. "And now we have no place to go."

"Mama, I would not worry about this too much. Kinmen is only few miles from the mainland, but Taiwan is more than one hundred miles away. Our navy is much stronger, and they have no air force yet," I said, trying to comfort her.

"I hope you are right. I hate the war. It causes so much killing and destruction and never achieves anything good," Mama said. Old memories must have haunted her.

"Mama, I think things will get better now. I assure you we are safe here," I said, but deep in my mind, I too was very worried. What if our navy and air force defected to the Reds as our troops did on the mainland? I did not say it to Mama.

In the following days, we were listening to the radio broadcast at home, in school, and on the speakers on the street. At school, classes were conducted as usual, but the war was in everybody's mind. I didn't know what the Taiwanese classmates were thinking, but the few mainlanders in my class were all very worried.

"I think the Communists will attack Taiwan as soon as they take over Kinmen. There are no more places for us to retreat. If they

The Island Heaven

come, I will join the army to fight them," said Jian-Kuo Li, a stocky sixteen-year-old.

"They don't have the kind of military force to attack us across the Taiwan Strait. Our air force will blow them out of the water before they come to the range of our shore guns. I am not too worried about it," said Shi-Chen Hsu, a seventeen-year-old soccer star of the high school team.

"But what if they made it through the strait and landed here? What would you do?" Jian-Kuo asked.

"If they could land their troops here, I would pick up a gun and fight them too, but I don't think that will ever happen," Shi-Chen said.

"I sure hope you are right," I told Shi-Chen.

From the news broadcast, the battle was very fierce. Our defending forces were able to kill most of the attackers, right in the landing crafts before landing. The troops that landed could not penetrate our defense lines on Kinmen Island or on Machu Island. The battle did not last very long. In about three days, it was over. It was a total victory for the Nationalist defenders on the two small islands. We were so relieved when the news of the victory came. That critical battle had boosted the morale of the people on the island and increased our hope to win back the mainland. Although there were no celebrations, everybody felt a dark cloud over their heads had been lifted. Baba came home in very high spirits.

"We fought a beautiful battle on Kinmen. The forces of the Red Army were at least five times more than our defending forces, but our brave soldiers really put up a good fight. They killed numerous of them and captured thousands of them," Baba said. Then he gulped down his first cup of his favorite black tea as Mama, Wye-Gong, and I listened.

After the big win, we all felt much safer to live in Taiwan. That shadow of war suddenly went away from our minds. Life had returned to the way it was before the short battle. Now the more important thing in my life was to win ball games. In my class, there were two unusually tall fellows: Hsin-Yen Wu and Tsi-Yuan Tsao.

Both were six feet, three inches. They were taller than most of the people in Taiwan and were the tallest two in the whole school. The rest of us were between five feet, six inches and five feet, ten inches. At five feet, seven inches, the shortest player on the basketball team, I was included because I was a very accurate jump shooter. Our class team easily won the provincial high school championship and went on to win the high school championship in Kao-Shiung. But we did not want to stop at that point. Our ambition was to compete with the local business-industrial teams.

We gave our team the name of Mustang, because the name represented freedom, speed, and youthfulness—a most fitting description of our team. We were just first-semester sophomores and the oldest fellow in the team was only seventeen. Hsin-Yen played the center and Tsi-Yuan was the forward. Both had also quit the gang organization a short while ago. The two fellows were not only tall and agile but also very smart; without them, we could never make it. Our teammates all recognized they were the real reason our team was doing so well. Since I was a good long-distance jump shooter, the team leader put me at the guard position. We practiced for individual skills and team coordination every other evening after school for one hour. We beat the navy team, the customs team, and the Shore Defense Command team to win the city championship. Our classroom display case was crowded with all sorts of awards and plaques. The most treasured one was presented by the mayor for the citywide championship. For the bunch of sixteen- and seventeen-year-olds, it was the highest honor we had never even hoped for.

On the other hand, our class soccer team was only average in the school. We won some and lost some games, but we had a lot of fun playing it. I played the center guard, which always required running back and forth on the field. At sixteen and seventeen, it was not a problem for me at all.

At our age, all my classmates and friends in the compound were naturally interested in girls, but the society was very conservative. We were taught at home and in school to be very discrete in approaching the opposite sex. Among teenage boys, to be seen with a girl was viewed by peers as not honorable or as a sissy. Boys had to show that they were not interested in girls in order to be pure and strong. I followed the custom but thought it was more envious and against nature more than anything else. In Taiwan, there were very few coed high schools on the island, and there was none in Kao-Shiung. All of schools above the sixth grade were segregated schools. There was the provincial high school and the provincial girl's high school, both of which were prestigious in southern Taiwan. Then there were the second-tier high schools and the less prestigious ones. All students in all schools had to wear uniform and each school would have an insignia put on the uniform to identify the schools and the classes.

Schoolgirls in Kao-Shiung were dressed uniformly with shirt and black skirts from seventh to twelfth grades. They wore the ugliest hairstyle, which looked like a black helmet put on a pumpkin. None of them wore any makeup and I thought they were taught to hate boys. Occasionally, we could see a decent-looking girl on the street, but those were not in student uniforms. If any of us looked at any girls, we would be teased for at least a week by our classmates.

In school, with all the busy activities, we rarely had time to talk about girls. I supposed all boys at the high school age were driven by hormones and really liked girls, but no one openly showed serious interest in chasing any girls. As far as I knew, not a single classmate of mine had a girlfriend. If there was one such occasion, the whole school would know, and it would become big news. In other words, there was no such thing as dating in high school for boys. However, that did not apply to girls. Many high school girls were openly dating naval officers, air force pilots, and the like. The boys were aware of it, but no one was showing any envy or emotions about it.

We had quite a few fictitious pairs among my classmates, but they were all created from thin air. It was more of a fun thing and material to tease the few docile classmates in the school. Through my high school years, I did not even talk to a single high school girl. Partly because there were no opportunities, and I never tried to seek such encounter either. Just about all my classmates were in the same situation. One of the reasons was the traditional education at home and the martial arts indoctrinations we were exposed to from very young ages. It was said a man must not get close to females in order to be pure, healthy, and strong. I was confident to say that ninety-nine out of one hundred boys had no close relationship with any girls when they graduated from high schools in Taiwan.

Here was one exception of the norm. One of my classmates, Shee-Tsan Hsu, bragged to one of his buddies about his intimate experiences with several girls. Soon everybody in class knew about it. Partly due to ignorance and partly due to the scare about the venereal disease, everybody in the class treated him like a plague and to be avoided. Whether it was true or not, no one bothered to find out. This fellow had lost his reputation and was to be abandoned by everyone. Nobody would shake hands or get close to him in the school. Poor Shee-Tsan graduated from high school without having a classmate as friend. All resulted from his bragging about the wrong thing. From what I knew, it was likely he just bragged or kidded with his buddies. Poor soul!

At school I was hired without pay to repair instruments in the physics laboratory. For some reason, not one classmate of mine had any interest in radio and electronics. The only friend who shared my hobby was Ru-Kao, while Yu-Si would just follow us around when we were out searching for electronics parts. My experiments with crystal radios were passed on to Ru-Kao and Yu-Si. We soon advanced to single vacuum tube radios and then to multiple tube radios. The hobby soon became an obsession to me. There was the big tin-roof building with a maze of antennas about half a mile from the living compound. I found out it was the intelligence and communication center for the US forces in Taiwan since the end of the war. The Dumpster in the back of the building was a major source of my collection of electronic parts, circuit boards, vacuum tubes, and broken electronic chassis. Other sources included street vendors and military surplus yards. Ru-Kao, Yu-Si, and I would team up to go to the military junkyard, where communication trucks and tanks were awaiting to be melted down for metals. We talked to the guards to allow us to disassemble them for small electronics parts.

"Sergeant, good morning. We are students from provincial high school. We need some electronic parts for experiment. Could we go in there and take them off the trucks?" I asked the young sergeant.

"This is a military yard. Civilians are not allowed in there. Just where are you come from?" He looked us over and asked.

"We are from Si-Tze Bay military compound. Our parents work for the Shore Defense Command," Ru-Kao told the sergeant.

"Oh! In that case, you are in the military family. I guess it is all right for you to go in there. We have no use for those junk parts anyway."

We went in the giant yard and climbed into the ransacked communication trucks. They were cannibalized by the military but left a great amount intact in the trucks. It was a bonanza for the two of us. We spent two hours collecting parts on the floors and small, unknown pieces disassembled from the walls and cabinets. Yu-Si helped us working on the disassembly. When walked out to the gate, the sergeant just waved us through. We went back there once every two weeks until one day we found all the communication trucks were hauled away to the ironwork to become steel ingots. In the yard, Yu-Si found a few rusty US Marine fighting knives and took them home.

"Yu-Si, what are you going to do with these knives?" I asked.

"These are the best fighting knives in the world. During World War II, every US Marine was carrying one to the battlefield. I have been looking for one since the war was over," Yu-Si said.

"I hope you won't use it to fight with people," Ru-Kao said.

"Of courec not. I will just use it to scare some bad guys. That's all," he said.

"Well, you want to be very careful with weapons like that, all right?" Ru-Kao warned him.

After we went home, Yu-Si worked very hard for two days, using sandpaper to sand off the rust on these knives. He gave Ru-Kao and me each a nice knife and kept the other two. He also showed them off to other kids in the compound. Everyone was envious of his fighting knives.

However, fighting knife was not something I was interested. My hobby was strictly radio and electronics. I would search for them in the junkyard or buy them from street vendors. But the military junkyard was closed after the broken tanks were removed. The only source I had then was the market. Since Mama never gave me an allowance for buying electronic parts, I had to save my lunch money to buy these "treasures." My lunch was limited to the cheapest food: the bananas. Months later, my stomach would become upset whenever I saw a banana.

My room became a laboratory and storage for my electronics. Mama became less tolerant to the "junk" littered everywhere, in addition to my own room.

"Ren look at the junk you pile in your room and in the hallways. The whole house is now a junkyard. How about throwing away the stuff you don't need and making some room for us?" said Mama, and she was not smiling.

"Fine, Mama. I will take care of it tomorrow," I promised.

"If you don't do something about it, I will help you to get rid some of them."

Reluctantly, I carted out several large boxes of things and took them to the Dumpster behind the American communications center.

A distant uncle, Pu Lin, the one Mama told me in Ma-Wei was a graduate of that naval academy, now was an admiral in command of Taiwan's amphibious fleet. When he heard that I collected electronic parts, he brought his five-tube radio to my house when he was visiting with Baba one day.

"This is fairly new radio, but it doesn't work. If you can fix it, you can keep it," Uncle Pu said.

"Wow! It is a five-tube radio. The new super heterodyne system. Thank you very much. Sure, you don't want it back if I fix it?" I was overwhelmed by such generosity.

"That's what I said. You can keep it," he said as he smiled broadly.

It was truly the greatest thing I had ever had. In the past, I had never owned a factory-manufactured radio. The only radios I had were the ones I made and the most advanced one was a three-tube radio mounted on the surface of a wood board.

While Uncle Pu was still talking to Baba in the living room, I took it apart and put it back together again several times, replacing several suspicious parts in the radio. It finally worked. I did find out what was wrong with it by replacing one component at a time. When the radio blurted out the loud music, I rushed to the living room to tell Uncle Pu about it.

"The radio is working now. It had one bad capacitor in the amplifier stage. I replaced it and it works like new," I said.

"It is yours now, and don't tell me anything about the 'capacitators.' I know nothing about any of it. Have fun with it," Uncle Pu told me before he returned to his conversation with Baba.

With that five-tube radio in my "laboratory," I believed it was the most disassembled and reassembled radio on earth. Each day I would take it apart to replace components from tubes to resistors, experimenting on the effect to the quality of the sound. All the work was done on a trial-and-error basis since I had no knowledge in its theoretical aspects, but I became very familiar with home radio repairs at the age of sixteen. Quickly, the word went out and I became a very busy free radio repairman for friends at school and in the compound. Soon the whole school staff found out about my abilities to repair radios and electrical instruments. The head teacher of physics gave me the responsibility as the school physics laboratory technician in charge of maintaining all electronics equipment. There was no pay whatsoever and I never even gave a thought about getting paid. What I gained was the learning opportunities and the fun associated with working with electronic test equipment in the laboratories.

At home, I also worked on different experiments for practical applications. At that time, special batteries for radio receivers and transmitters were very expensive, and they ran out of power very quickly. I had been experimenting with all types of rectifiers and power conversion circuits and made several versions of power supplies to power my different electronic projects.

I visited the communication detachment at the north end of the beach to visit Lieutenant Ku, one of the basketball buddies for the kids in the compound. He was overseeing a few radio transmitter/receiver units and constantly monitored the radio traffic of the Red Army. It was quite an impressive place for me to see. I also saw two soldiers sitting on a stool and cranking the generator constantly.

"Why do you have to use the hand-cranked generators to power the units?" I was curious.

"Well, the batteries, especially the high-voltage ones, are very expensive. We must import them from the United States, so I just use the generator to save money. We have a lot of manpower here," he said, and he let out a short laugh.

"If I make a power supply for you, would you like to try it out?" I asked.

"Sure, as long as it will not burn up my equipment. Otherwise, bang!" He used his hand to signal a pistol shooting at his head.

"I will make sure it will not harm your equipment. Besides, we need you to play basketball on our team," I assured him.

Lieutenant Ku gave me the power supply requirement of the unit for reference. I went home and used surplus parts I bought from the market and made a power supply to replace the batteries for his radio transmitter-receiver units. I delivered the power supply unit about three days later at his outfit.

"Gee, it sure looks ugly, but does it work?" he asked me.

"I have tested it many times at home. It works for my radios. Are you willing to try it out?" I asked as I detected the reluctance on his face.

"All right, I will let you try on this older unit, but be careful." He was still very, very nervous about ruining the government property. But I knew the power supply I made would never do any harm to the units.

I hooked the power supply wires to the unit and then plugged it into the city power outlet. With the radio off, there was no smoke coming out from anything. He felt better and then he switched on the radio. The dial panel lit up and a voice blurted out. He was so relieved by this time.

"How about sending out a test transmission and seeing if your contact can receive it?" I asked. I was confident it would not burn up. He sat down and used Morse code to send out a minute-long signals; still no smoke was seen. Two minutes later, the new frequency he had set received the Morse code reply.

He didn't tell me what it said, but Lieutenant Ku was so happy. He shook my hand and thanked me, then he said, "I have six units here. How about make five more for me? I will pay for the cost of the parts."

"No problem. I will make five more for you. The surplus parts did not cost me much money, so you don't have to pay me anything. But if you run into any junked radio equipment, please let me know." I had my eyes on the retired equipment.

"I don't have anything now, but when we have any obsolete equipment, I will try to get it for you," he said.

"Great, that's a deal. I will need two weeks to get the power supplies done," I promised him.

About ten days later, I delivered the units two and three at a time and set them up for the soldiers. All the radio units worked well with the home-made power supplies. There was no more need for soldiers to crank the generators.

By using my homemade power supplies to replace the batteries, the lieutenant had saved a lot of money for his army unit. Because of this big saving, when Taiwan's economy was very tight, he was awarded a medal by his commanding general in a ceremony. Lieutenant Ku, in turn, bought me a big order of crushed-ice drink to celebrate. Both of us were very happy that day.

Living on the seashore had the advantages of getting to the fishing spot in just a few minutes. I fished at my favorite fishing spot almost daily and always wore my swimming trunks, alternating between fishing and swimming. My fishing hole was inside the concrete wave-barrier. I had a rock as my stool. Since I was never serious at catching any fish, I threw all the fish I caught back to the ocean and just went home empty-handed, unlike during the war; we no longer needed the kind of small fish I caught for food.

The Shore Defense Command gave net-fishing permission to a group of twenty or so professional fishermen from the city to catch fish from the beach. When the group of fishermen was on the beach, armed guards were placed nearby to watch them closely. The fishermen would work there for two months in late spring two or three times per week. I was recruited by the fishermen to help them pull the net in after the fishing boat had dropped the drag net in the ocean about two hundred yards out. Two teams of about ten persons were pulling at each end of the net and slowly towed the net toward the shore. It took about half an hour to get the net completely onshore. The net became heavier as it got closer to the shore. Of course, when it was heavy, it meant to have more catch. To show their appreciation for my help, the fishermen would give me a few pounds of fish to take home. It was more than enough fish for my family for the entire week. Therefore, when I was sitting on the rock, casting the rod was purely for fun.

Because the weather was mild year-round, and the seashore was only minutes away, I dipped into the sea two or three times a day for at least ten months per year. At the time, in the early 1950s, we all believed that sunbathing was good for the health and the darker the skin the more handsome it was for boys. When we first moved into the compound, none of the kids knew how to swim, but in a matter of just a month, all the boys became good swimmers. Our skin was burned into dark-brown color. Each month we might shed once or twice the burned skin. It simply peeled off like a layer of thin wax paper.

Teenagers from the compound and friends from the city (we had to escort them into the restricted area) were competing in all sorts of swimming techniques and water-related games. One was diving without any support and seeing how long one could stay underwater. This was the only contest that I could beat all of others in. Among all the boys, Ru-Kao was the best in swimming skills, whether it was diving from a rock or it was the speed contest. Ru-Kao was a year younger than me. He was also an electronics junkie, a good friend, and a faithful follower of mine in many new ventures.

The seawater was very salty. Many people could not open their eyes in the seawater. Only a few of the kids, including me, could open our eyes underwater for a minute or more without any protection. In the beginning, it was painful to the eyes, but after a few days, I was totally accustomed to it. Minor mishaps occurred from time to time, such as cuts and injuries to the swimmers. Nothing major happened to any of the kids in the compound through the years.

One day, a boy from the city came with Tsan-Mou and dove from the rock where we always did. The spot was full of huge rocks. We had to be careful to dive into the water where there was an opening between two giant rocks. For some unfortunate reasons, this one dive he made cracked his skull. He did not come up for longer than usual. Ru-Kao dove in to pull him out of the water. He was bleeding and unconscious. We rushed him to the local hospital, but it was too late. He died on the way to the hospital in the military Jeep. We all were scared by that incident. From that day on, no one ever dove from that rock again. Looking back, I found that we indeed had done many very foolish things.

CHAPTER 7

DROWNING AFTER A TYPHOON

On the island, people were feared of earthquakes, but the major epicenters were in the eastern cities, especially near Hwa-Lian and southern cities like Tai-dong. The damages to Kao-Shiung, hundreds of miles away, were much less than to cities near the epicenters. I had experienced at least twenty strong earthquakes in the past year while at home or in the school, but there were no casualties other than some damage to poorly constructed houses. Now when I felt the quake was coming, I would not even bother to move to an open area.

Another threat to residents was the Pacific storm; we called it typhoon. I had heard about typhoons but the ones that came in the past year landed in faraway cities, so the impact was minimal to us. We had some strong winds, broken braches, and heavy rains that were the kind of typhoon strength I knew—nothing too threatening. However, one late afternoon in July, there was a warning on the radio that a strong typhoon was coming toward this area and might land near Kao-Shiung. I understood this time it might be different from what I had experienced in the past.

"Mama, a strong typhoon is coming. The radio says it is going to be landing near here. Should we go somewhere to find stronger shelter?" I heard the warning and the advice for people to seek shelter.

"I think we will be fine. The house is new, and we are behind the big mountain, so wind will be weakened when it gets here." Mama was not worried at all.

"I think I will go to the bunker on the east end of the guardhouse. They know me well." Wye Gong was thinking about playing cards with his buddies in the bunker.

"Daddy, if you want to go there, you'd better go before the wind comes. How about you eat supper alone first?" Mama told Wye-Gong.

"I think I will just do that." Wye-Gong went ahead to eat and left the house.

I stayed on monitoring the radio and looking outside for signs of the anticipated typhoon. It was quite dark for a summer afternoon. The clouds were thick, dark, and moving fast in a direction from the east. Since we had the Sou Mountain on the east of the compound, the wind was not so strong at that moment. Baba came at about six o'clock and did not seem to be worried about the pending typhoon.

"Baba, I heard the typhoon is going to a big one and may hit us directly," I said.

"If the typhoon is landing north of Kao-Shiung, we will be fine, but if it lands at the south, we will just have some east wind that is blocked by the mountain. The worst case would be to have the eye of typhoon passing through here, then we will be hit hard after the eye has passed here—from the west side," Baba said.

"If that is the case, what should we do?" I asked.

"We will not know it until it lands. By then, it would be too late for us to find a shelter, but the chance to have a direct hit is rare here." Baba was quite confident.

"Baba, if it should land here, what do we do?" I insisted.

"Well, the best we can do is to find a spot in the house that will not collapse when the wind becomes very strong. I would stay in the opposite end of the house when the storm comes from the west." Baba pointed toward the master bedroom.

As we sat down eating supper, the wind started hawing and whistling but did not sound any worse than other storms we had before. The radio broadcast was not giving any new information. I was hoping the storm would land north of here and then bypass Kao-Shiung. That evening was relatively quiet, but I was awakened by the pulsating, rushing sound mixed with whistling. At times, I thought the house was moving. The roof joints made such crackling noise at each rush of the wind, I was afraid the house was going to be blown apart. I got up and heard Mama and Baba were up in the living room with a candle on the table. The electricity was cut off. I assumed the downed trees might have broken the power lines. The rain was hitting the house horizontally. Water leaked in from windowsills and gaps between the door and frame. A huge, shallow puddle formed right inside the door.

"Baba, this sounds like the typhoon has landed in the area, doesn't it?" I asked.

"I don't know. I have never experienced a direct hit by a typhoon. The wind apparently is from the east side, and it is not good news," Baba said. He inhaled the cigarette smoke deeply and then slowly puffed it out. Windows were shaking as if they would implode at any time.

"Baba, this room is facing east. Maybe we should go to my room, which is at the west side. I think it is safer there," I suggested.

"You are right. If the wind changes the direction, then we will come back here."

We took the candle to my room and made our ways through the piles of "junk." I asked Baba and Mama to sit on the bed and I just milled around try to find out where had I put my earphones. I hadn't touched the crystal radio since I started working on vacuum tube radios. I finally found it and hooked it to my crystal set. The radio station was still broadcasting. I knew they had emergency power system for the station. I tuned to the news station and the news confirmed our suspicion.

"Baba, the news says the typhoon had landed near Kao-Shiung from the southeast. That means the eye will be coming this way?" I asked.

"We will know that when and if it comes this way. Because at the eye, there be no wind and we will have a moment of quietness. Behind the eye, we will be on the other side of the storm and the wind will reverse its direction," Baba said. "Your crystal radio is more superior to our big radio. It works when the power is out."

"Let me listen to the news," Baba told me. That was the first time he listened to my crystal radio. "Ah! The typhoon will pass through here. We'd better be prepared. Why don't you all put on heavy clothes and wear a cap to protect from the cold and debris just in case?"

"Is it that serious?" Mama said as she got up to find extra clothes for Baba and herself. I also went to the closet to get my heavy jacket and a hat to wear. The temperature had dropped when the storm came so with the extra clothing, I did not feel too warm. I tried to look outside. It was pitch-dark, and I could not see a thing. The howling wind sounded much fierce than earlier. The ceiling was moving slightly toward the west as the gusts of wind pushed from the east side.

"Do you think the house can stand the pressure of the gusts?" Mama asked Baba. She had been quite scared, since this was her first encounter with such a strong storm.

"It has been more than one hour since the main storm hit. The house is doing fine. We will be safe here," After another hour or so, suddenly, the wind and rain both stopped. Baba said.

"The typhoon's eye is passing here. I am more worried about the westward wind where we don't have anything between us and the storm. Let us be ready just in case the house is blown apart," Baba said as he got up to check other parts of the house. He then told Mama that there was no damage to the house at this time. He found a long wood board and used it to reinforce the door facing the west.

"Move everything away from the windows, and there might be water come in the house. Anything you want to keep dry should be lifted off the floor," Baba told me and then Mama. "Maybe we have time to make some tea before the storm hits again."

"Let me heat up some water in the charcoal stove," she said as she went to the kitchen. Normally she would be using an electric stove, but the power was cut off. The city water was also cut so she just poured the hot water from the thermo pot and reheated it in order to make tea. I was busy moving my treasured "junk" onto my bed and the table from the floor.

Just when Baba was drinking the hot tea, the wind speed picked up. This time, it was the opposite of the direction a little while ago and the force increased suddenly and not gradually. The rain now hit the west side doors and window, forcing water into the house. Baba and Mama now stayed in the master bedroom at the northeast corner of the house where Baba said it would be the safest place. I also went in the room and sat on a chair.

The wind and rain bombarding the house relentlessly sometimes felt like a boxer's punch: one, two, and three in quick session. We sat there silently listening to the crackling noise on the roof joints and the crashing sound of objects smashing against each other or hitting the ground near the house.

I felt my feet were very cold. When I paid attention to the floor, I found the room had two inches of water. The water had forced through the gaps of the door and the windows. I walked to the other side of the house; the water was deeper and flowed to the lowest point of the house, which was the shower room. Fortunately, it had a drain to lead the water out of the house.

"Mama, the whole house has water on the floor, but nothing is broken so far!" I yelled loudly enough so Mama could hear me. Back into my room, the noise sounded much louder. The rain was like thousands of sand pebbles hitting on the glass windows, wave after wave. I felt the windows could cave in if a stronger gust should come and if a window was broken, the whole house would be blown into pieces like an explosion. I was scared, but there was nothing I could do to prevent it.

Baba sat on the side of the bed with a pot of tea on the nightstand. His cigarettes had not required a match since we woke up to the storm. A pile of cigarette butts was in the ashtray. Mama blew the candle out.

"This is the only candle I have. I want to keep it when I really need to use it," she said.

"Well, if the house is blown over, you will never need it again," Baba said.

We then just sat in the dark quietly. When Baba smoked, the cigarette was the brief source of light for me to see objects in the room. The storm suddenly subsided as it came. The room became very quiet, although we still could hear the rain and blowing winds.

"Ah! I believe the storm is over. I am glad they built the house well enough to sustain the typhoon," Baba told Mama. "It is almost daylight. Why don't we go back to rest for a while?"

"I am tired too. I will sleep in Wye-Gong's bed," I said, because my bed was occupied by my electronics collections.

When I woke up that morning, it was almost nine o'clock. I rushed to clean myself and went to check the outside. I saw Tsan-Mou and Yu-Si standing in the yard and went to join them.

"Are you guys going to school today? I am sure it is closed," I said.

"I am sure the morning classes are closed, but the afternoon may resume normal operations," Yu-Si said. "Have you seen the damages to this area?"

"No, I just got up," I replied.

"We have been up since six. You should see that great big tin-roof building used by American communications detachment that was blown apart. The metal roof was lifted and blown more than a hundred feet from the rest of the building. The building was totally demolished, and debris spread over a hundred square yards," Yu-Si said.

"I want to look around the shore area. Do you like to go with me?" I asked.

They both agreed. The three of us walked toward the beach through debris, broken tree branches, and several uprooted tall trees. On the shore, we could see the contour of the sand beach was altered by the storm. Although the wind had died down, the waves were still very high. The water crashed onto the huge rocks at the north end, sounding like explosions. No one else was seen on the beach.

"How about let's go to school and see what happened there?" Yu-Si asked.

"Why don't we go? We don't have anything else to do anyway," Tsan-Mou said.

"All right, I will get some lunch money from my mom then we go. How about we met here in ten minutes?" I suggested. The two agreed.

We walked through the darkened tunnel out to the street. The ground and the street outside of the tunnel were full of broken branches, debris, and some fallen trees, but the bus was still operating. We arrived at the school in late morning; many students were already there. Someone told us to go home because the school was closed for the day. We walked to the campus and found the giant tree, which was the symbol of the age of the school, had been uprooted, fell toward the building, and squarely blocked the entrance to the administration building. A notice to close the school was posted right next to the entrance. Several temporary structures behind the classroom building were also severely damaged. The three of us decided to go home right away.

Yu-Si had been my closest friend inside the compound, and he was a nice and gentle fellow. He was six feet, two inches tall and 170 pounds. I was five feet, seven inches and 125 pounds. We were born in the same year, but I was two months of his senior. We lived only sixty feet apart in two different duplexes. Since we moved into the compound, we had been friends. Yu-Si seemed to have a little problem with his slow waking up after a night of sleep. Each morning I routinely went to Yu-Si's house, woke him up, and got him dressed in sporting shorts. He would just follow me jogging to the exercise field. Every morning after we jogged for about two or three minutes on the road, he would ask me, "Where are we going?" He was not yet quite awake.

"We are going to the field to exercise," I had to remind him.

"Oh!" he would say.

At first, I thought he was joking, but later it was apparent to me that he was quite serious about his questions. It would take another few minutes before he became fully awake. I thought it was strange because I was fully awake in the morning the minute, I opened my eyes. I knew there were differences in people and never gave much attention to Yu-Si's slow waking-up symptoms.

In school, Yu-Si was a slow learner, but he was very knowledgeable with current news and events and was very popular with schoolmates. He entered the high school as a seventh grader, and I was in the ninth grade. He was still an eighth grader when I was in the eleventh grade. I thought he did not study hard enough. So, I tried to help him with his homework and went over some subjects he had just learned from the classes. He was very smart on social issues, but he just could not remember any numbers and any analytical subjects. He always tried to hide his deficiency and did a good job in that. I did not know he had problems until one day while we were waiting for the bus to school.

"Hey! Yu-Si, what time do you have?" I asked.

"Seven thirty," he said, looking at his watch.

"It can't be. We left the house just a few minutes ago. It was six twenty. Your watch must be off," I said.

I grabbed his wrist to check it. Indeed, it was only six forty-five. It was then I discovered that he did not even know how to read a timepiece at the age of seventeen. I felt very bad, but I did not know how to help him. I tried to teach him how to read the watch, but without any success. After I went home that day, I consulted with my mother.

"Mama, I think Yu-Si has some real learning problems. He is not dumb, but he just can't get through his head about schoolwork. I am worried for him," I said.

"Well, his mother told me when he was six years old, he was ill with very high fever. The illness may have damaged part of his brain, I think." Mama was worried for this poor young man as well.

"I wonder if there is any medicine, he can take to help his memory." I really wished there was something that might help him.

"I don't know if there is such medicine," Mama said. She shook her head with a very somber expression. In the meantime, I thought I should try to help him in school and keep company as a friend.

It was the day after that strong typhoon had passed Kao-Shiung. The sky was cloudless and bright. The school was still closed, and the houses were still out of water and electricity. I played with my collections of electronic parts for a while and could not find anything better to do in the home, because without electric power, I just could not do anything with my radios. I thought it would be cool to dip in the strong waves after the typhoon and see how it felt by standing in the mist of the big waves. It would be more fun to have my buddy to go with me, so I went to Yu-Si's home. He was sitting there reading newspapers.

"What are you doing at home in a day like this? Let us go and see how the ocean is doing after typhoon," I said to him.

He put down the newspaper, got up, and said, "All right, let's go."

We walked to the seashore and watched the reshaped terrain of the sand beach. At this moment, the wind had subsided to almost a mild breeze. And the sun came out, heating up the beach. The heat, the humidity, and the cool water made the idea of dipping in the seawater ever inviting.

"It is so hot now. How about let's dip in the waves?" I said to Yu-Si.

"Are you crazy? You know. It's very dangerous after typhoon, and if you get caught, you would be in real trouble with the guards here too," he replied in disbelief.

"Look. We will just go in the shallow part of the water and swim sideways. That should be all right. We will not swim to the deep water, I assure you. Besides whom would be out here to catch swimmers today, anyway?" I tried to convince him.

"All right remember we will only go to the shallow water," Yu-Si reluctantly agreed.

We did not wear our shoes to the beach when we left the house. We took off our T-shirts and slowly walked into the water. It really was not so bad. The waves were quite a bit higher than usual, but it was not something we had not seen before. But after standing in the water, I thought if we swam in the shallow water it would very safe.

"Yu-Si follow me and swim sideways along the shore, and keep a close distance with me," I said. "You swim inside so I can help you if you need it," I said, because I was a much stronger swimmer than him.

"I will be right beside you," he said. Apparently, he felt quite safe with the low wind and in the shallow water.

Because the sand beach slope was very gradual, we had to walk out almost fifty feet in the water before we reached the depth of four feet in the water. At that point, the wave was no more than six feet high. Only when an occasional big wave came, we could not touch the sand with our feet.

"It's not so bad. Is it?" I said to Yu-Si.

"Yeah, I still don't feel good about this," he said.

"Don't worry. Let's enjoy the waves. Remember don't swim too far from me," I told him.

We started at about fifty feet off the water line on the beach and swam along the shoreline for about ten minutes. Suddenly, we both found that we were washed toward the ocean by the retreating tides (riptide) and were then more than one hundred yards from the shore in that short time. We immediately knew we were in big trouble, that the force of the retreating tides was carrying us out to the sea at a high rate of speed. Yu-Si tried to reach the sand under him but found the water was too deep. The speed of the retreating tide was so high that we had to overcome the force by swimming fast toward the shore.

"Yu-Si, we are being washed out to the sea. Let's swim toward the shore as fast as we can right now," I told him.

"I know. This is very bad," he said as he started swimming toward the shore.

We swam toward the beach for a few minutes but judging from the distance between the shore and us, we were not making any progress at all; we were washed farther out. I was concerned but not frightened at that moment. I thought we could swim faster than the tide that could carry us out.

"Yu-Si, let's race to the shore." I tried to make that a challenge to him, thinking we always swam faster when we raced.

Yu-Si only agreed by nodding his head.

The two of us continued struggled very hard to swim faster toward the shore, but obviously we were washed farther out to the sea. After trying for about half an hour, it appeared to us it was hopeless to swim back to shore. We were both exhausted by swimming fast against the tide. Yu-Si had slowed down and went behind me. So, I swam back to be with him.

"I don't want to die. I know we are going to die!" Yu-Si was very upset and started crying.

"Yu-Si, listen, we are getting tired. Just swim on your back slowly to conserve your energy. Maybe the tide will change direction soon," I told him. We both flipped over to backstroke and swam slowly and aimlessly.

"You know we are going to be drowned. What is the use to fool ourselves?" Yu-Si was not all optimistic.

"Please do not give up until we can't move anymore. But if we don't make it, I want to let you know that you have been the best friend of mine. I am sorry to get you into this mess," I said.

"This is all set in our fate. It was meant to happen like this as the end for both of us," Yu-Si said, turning his head around toward me. I was tired and felt hopeless.

"Yu-Si, good-bye. See you in the next life," I said. I was so tired that I thought the end was coming soon.

"Good-bye!" he said, waving his hand. I waved back at him.

We continued to keep afloat on our backs, but we drifted apart unintentionally.

A surge of sadness hit me very hard. I thought about what would happen when Mama and Baba found that their only child was drowned. I did not weep, but I know my tears were welling in my eyes when I thought about them. Many events in the past quickly flashed through my mind. Things I had done, words I had said, people I loved and hated all presented like movie frames in quick session. There were regrets and comforts for what I did. Now that I was going to leave everything behind, I just wished I could do a few things differently. I wished I had been a better son for my parents. I wished I had not disobeyed Mama so often, and my attitude was often quite bad. I wished I had not caused so much trouble for Mama as she brought me up in those terribly difficult situations during the war. I wished I had been kinder toward some of my classmates I thought were weaklings. I felt a big comfort to recall how happy and proud Mama and Baba were when I brought the first report card that said I was the number 1 in the class just a year ago. I also wished I hadn't killed my next-door neighbor's cock accidentally with my slingshot when I was ten. Many other thoughts just flashed through my mind while I swam slowly on my back without paying attention to where I was going.

As we were exhausted by the lengthy physical struggle and became disoriented, instead of swimming toward the shore, we were swimming sideways along the shore. It must have been ten minutes after we said good-bye when suddenly I heard a faint voice in the loud noise of waves. Yu-Si was calling me excitedly, a short distance away. "Tien-Ren, look! I am standing on the sand here." He was standing on a sandbar some twenty yards away from me, in chest deep water. He was on the south side of where I was and farther out toward the ocean. The typhoon had rearranged the shape of the sandbar underwater. A new island had formed like an underwater pier straight from the shore toward the ocean. I knew what happened might be our only hope to get back to the shore. I swam toward Yu-Si and stood up. I found I could stand on the sand with my head out of the water when the wave was low.

"We are saved!" I said. "Let's walk back to the shore."

"Thank god!" Yu-Si said with all sincerity.

We walked toward the shore, saying nothing to each other because we were so tired. It felt like forever for us to reach the dry beach. After we were on the dry sand, both of us collapsed on the sand and fell asleep before we could say anything again. By the time we woke up, it was very dark at night.

"Yu-Si, I am sorry to get you into so much trouble and thank god we are still here. Please do not tell anybody else about this incident," I asked him.

"I swear to my honor! I will not tell anybody about what happened today," he promised.

When I got home, Mama thought I was playing basketball. I was so happy to see her. It was almost unreal and the whole world seemed so different to me; the house, the living room, and the kitchen all looked so dear to me, as if I had just come back from a long leave from a different planet.

"The food is cold now. Let me heat up the dishes for you," Mama said.

"Mama, I will eat now. You don't have to heat it up," I told Mama. She did not know how close it was that I might not be able to make it home that day—and forever!

This experience had taught me something that I had never realized. People could lose their lives at any moment without warning or fanfare. I was on the verge of losing it and I regained it back—accidentally. My life from that day on was a gift of second chance and I deeply appreciated it. We all came here just once. What is more precious than life itself? I vowed that I would change my philosophy toward life and matters. I would never put gains or losses of matters above personal well-being of others. I wanted to review what I did in the past and revise my attitude toward people. I would not do anything that I might regret later. I believe I grew older at least by ten years from that fateful afternoon in the ocean. Mama and Baba never learned about the event until forty year later. When I told them the story, they were still shocked by how close it was losing their only child.

The drowning incident has impacted my life in a very subtle way. The incident rarely came back to my mind. However, when I encountered difficult situations or making heavy decisions, I would think about that day and everything became so insignificant compared with what might have happened to me. I believe I have changed and become a gentler and more considerate person since that day.

CHAPTER 8

CRITICAL DECISIONS

The most admired teacher in all my school experiences was the physics teacher in my senior year. Capitan Hsiu was an active duty air force officer whose base was just thirty-five minutes of bicycle riding from the high school. He had the permission from his base commander to teach a one-hour afternoon class Monday through Saturday. He was an electrical engineering staff member of the air force and was not a pilot. Therefore, his working hours were more flexible. He was truly very well versed with the subjects in physics. He was always well prepared in classes. He never brought any textbook to the class, and he knew every topic in the book and much more. He was confident, patient, and thorough in teaching and answering any questions. I thought he was the best teacher I had ever had. If I would teach classes one day in the future, I would like to make him my role model. We had him for just one semester. He was transferred to another air force base in northern Taiwan right after the first semester ended. That transfer took place during the semester break. We did not even have a chance to say good-bye to him. We all felt it was a great loss of not having him as our physics teacher to finish our senior year. Our new physics instructor was just an average teacher, by contrast. We gave him a lot of hard times in the classroom. The poor guy did not even know where all the resentment came from.

I had been amazed with flying since I was ten years old. When the air force recruiters came to recruit senior classes in the high school, I was among the fifty or so students who responded. After several days of test and screening, only four students were accepted to the air force academy: Chuan-Hsu Yeh, Kwai-San Wang, Shi-Chen Hsu, and me. I was so happy about it and told Mama the minute I saw her at home.

"Mama, I was accepted by the air force academy. In the entire school, they only accepted four of us," I said excitedly.

"I am glad for you and very proud about your acceptance, but I don't know if I like it," Mama said with a somber face.

At first, I didn't know what to make of it, because this was an honor for me. But then I realized she was worried about the danger involved in flying a fighter plane, and there was still a war between mainland and Taiwan. I had heard rumors about bombing missions by our air force in cities of mainland China.

"But Mama, it is not as dangerous as you think. Nowadays the planes are much better made and maintained. I have not heard of a single military plane crash since we moved here." I tried to convince her.

"Well, son, those things were not publicized and kept secret to people here. I was told several of those accidents happened in the last few months alone." Mama was still unmoved.

When Baba came home, Mama told him about our discussions of the news.

"Son, if you really want to become an air taxi driver, go ahead," Baba said with a tone of disapproval. I then was torn between leaving my parents worrying for the safety of their only child and fulfilling my desire to fly. After several days of being torn between the two choices, I decided to decline the offer from the air force.

"Why in the world do you want to decline this opportunity to become a pilot?" Kwai-San asked me after I told him my decision.

The Island Heaven

"Well, as the only child in the family, I don't have the heart to worry my parents." I told him the truth, but his disbelief to my justification was written on his face.

"I think you are chickening out, aren't you?" He looked at me from the side of his eyes. "Well, that's your future. I was hoping we could be flying together."

"I am sorry, but I will be watching you when you get up there," I said.

Kwai-San was on both the soccer team and the basketball team. He was an orphan who came with an army officer who took him into the military and then sent him to school. He had lost contact with his uncles on the mainland and had no knowledge what had happened to them. He was a well-known daredevil in the school. Once in a fire drill, the fire department official asked who was willing to jump from the third floor of the building to demonstrate a fire rescue skill. The only volunteer was Kwai-San. With the whole school watching, he jumped into the ten-foot by ten-foot canvas without any hesitations. Like Kwai-San, the other two fellows were also moved to Taiwan with relatives or with the military when they escaped the mainland.

Until this day, I had been with Mama all my life and had never been separated from her. Just before the starting of the last semester in my senior year in high school, Baba was transferred to the Army General Headquarters in Taipei as a department head in the G2 section (intelligence). Mama and Baba had to move to Taipei immediately, but I had to stay in Kao-Shiung to finish my last semester in high school. I could not stay alone in the same house since it was immediately assigned to another official of the command. To place me in the city alone was not easy, because we didn't have the kind money to pay people for room and board.

After some searching, Baba arranged for me to stay with one of his friends, Major Chan, from the same command. Mrs. Chan owns a restaurant business in downtown Kao-Shiung on the second floor of the fresh-vegetable and meat market. The second-floor spaces were used for restaurants and bars. Mrs. Chan had one section on the second floor as the restaurant. The kitchen was in a room next to the dining room. There was no separated room set aside just for me. I had to put a bamboo-braided bed in this unused small storage room behind the kitchen right next to a bar with a wooden door that was nailed shut. The door was permanently sealed but the sound could still pass through the cracks and gaps between the door and the doorframe. Well, this would be a place for me just to sleep for the rest of three months. Shouldn't be a problem, I thought.

The day they left for Taipei; I went to the railway station to see them off. It was particularly hard for Mama. She repeatedly told me to keep warm, have enough to eat, and rest well. I told her not to worry. I was already a grown-up man at eighteen years old. Baba also told me to be careful and to write to them often. Before Mama departed at the train station, she stuffed a buddle of cash in my pocket and turned around while boarding the train. I knew she was crying.

I moved into the temporary shelter the day Baba and Mama left Kao-Shiung.

"Your father is my good friend. You should feel at home here. We have the restaurant here. I want you to eat here like a family and not to pay for anything. If there is anything else you need, just let me know," Major Chan told me.

Each morning, Mrs. Chan would get up early and prepare my breakfast for me. I was very moved by their hospitality. At first, I thought after midnight the restaurant business would be long closed. There would be no one in the kitchen and I should have a quiet place to myself for the night. Not so. The next-door bar was a place for night creatures. Every night after eleven, it would begin to get crowded by men and women. I could not see them, but the voice was loud and clear. The crazy noises made by American sailors and those bar girls were very annoying to me. I needed to study for my exams and the graduation test, so I had to study at night. This place certainly did not allow me to do so.

I found a Catholic Church-run library just two blocks down the street to study at night before going back to sleep after midnight. At school, I ate in the school cafeteria or bought food from street vendors. At night I did eat in Mrs. Chan's restaurant. Everything was just fine except for the bar next door. It was a brothel entertaining U.S. sailor from the Seventh Fleet. It had such loud music played all night long and the noises made by those sailors and bar girls bothered me infinitely. I did not want to hurt the feelings of the Chan family, so I just stayed on and kept my mouth shut.

One day in October, I woke up in the morning feeling very cold. I looked around and found the storage room was demolished. The window was gone; everything in the room was soaking wet. A strong typhoon had just passed through Kao-Shiung, and I slept through it. I was soaking wet. My books and everything else were also soaked in water. I finally had this excuse to move out of this noisy place. I remembered my classmate Rae-Chin Tseng was a big landlord in the city. I thought I might borrow one of the vacant apartments for a few days to give me time to find another place to live. Rae-Chin agreed without any hesitations. I moved into one apartment the same evening.

The uncle, Pu Lin, an admiral in the navy who had given me my first five-tube radio, was a brother-in-law of Mama's brother-in-law. He saw me in a bookstore by chance. When he chatted with me and found out my situation, he ordered his driver to drive me to my apartment room, pick up my belongings, and move me to his house in a navy-housing compound for ranking officers. He was still the admiral in charge of the amphibious fleet. The large house had a large attached garage. The garage was converted to a sleeping quarter. After talking to his wife, he sent me to move into the garage and stay with his brother-in-law, Han-Tung Chen, who married my mother's younger sister. I shared a bunker with Uncle Han-Tung. At night he coughed a lot, but it did not bother me since I was a deep sleeper.

"Uncle, you cough so much. Do you have a cold?" I asked.

"They didn't tell you! I have tuberculosis. It is beyond help now." He sighed, "Although you are young and healthy, I don't think it is good for you to stay so close to me."

"Thank you for telling me. I will move out as soon as I find a place to sleep," I said, and I was very angry and wondered why Uncle Pu would knowingly put me in such danger. They had plenty of rooms in the main house. Why wouldn't they let me use just a small corner in the house or simply not invite me to live with them at all? I had to do something about it. So, I bought a mask for my nose in order to reduce the chance of getting tuberculosis, but I knew it might not even be useful. I thought it was very uncomfortable and psychologically harmful to stay there. I still had about a month to go before my final examination, so I talked to Rae-Chin again. He found another vacant room for me. Two days after I found out Uncle Han-Dong had TB, I moved out of the garage without giving Uncle Pu any excuse. I was very mad at him for knowingly exposed me to a TB carrier that might have caused me to contract tuberculosis. I never told Mama and Baba about this matter because I knew what Baba might do to Uncle Pu.

All the problems associated with my temporary residences did not cause any problems for my schoolwork. I took the final examinations and maintained my grade average without any difficulty. The day after final examination, I got up at dawn and went to see Rae-chin to thank him.

"Rae-Chin, I am leaving for Taipei today. I want to thank you for helping me out in the last month. When I make money in the future, I will pay you back the rent and the friendship."

"Nonsense. You don't owe me anything, but just consider this our friendship. Come back and see us when you are back here in the future," Rae-Chin said with all sincerity.

After leaving Rae-Chin's house, I packed up my books and a small suitcase from the apartment and walked the thirty minutes to the railway station. There, I took a northbound train to join my parents in Taipei. The graduation ceremony was scheduled for a week later. I did not wait for my graduation. We did not have a phone in the house, and the only way to communicate with Mama and Baba in the past six months was by way of writing letters. The last five months was the first time I parted with Mama that long, and I missed her very much. It took the express train about eight hours to reach Taipei at four in the afternoon. Mama and Baba had a Jeep waiting for me at the train station. They knew my schedule a week earlier from the letter I wrote.

"Son, I am so glad to see you. You are looking fine after all these exams," Baba said, putting his hand on my shoulder. We climbed onto the Jeep. It was a three-quarter-ton Jeep with a canvas top. Baba was riding in the cab with the driver in the front cabin.

"Ren, you have lost some weight. Let me cook some good food for you to fill you up," Mama told me on the way home. She was apparently very happy to see me too.

"I am just fine, Mama. It is so good to see you and Baba, and I am very hungry for your food," I said.

The trip from the train station was only fifteen minutes. Baba helped me to carry my books while I took the suitcase inside the house. My heart was filled with joy, and I was very relaxed for the first time in six months. We moved into a rented house, sharing with four families in an enclosed high brick wall. It was located at the east end of the big city and was convenient to reach anywhere in the city by bus or bicycle. The only other big kid living inside the complex was a fourteen-year-old boy named Yiao-Hwa Shiung. A very intelligent fellow with a disproportional large head, I called him Big Head Shiung. The day we moved in, he approached me, and I was surprised by how mature and knowledgeable he was. We talked late into the night. There were other kids, but they were much younger.

Since I was graduating in December, all college entrance examinations were given in late June. I thought I had a lot of time in hand to study for college entrance examinations. There were very few colleges in Taiwan. Only a small percentage of high school graduates had the opportunity to enter colleges. Competition to enter a college was very keen but I knew that without a college degree, the future would be very dim. I planned to study very hard to take the entrance exams.

Unfortunately, as soon as I moved to Taipei, within two days, I was hit by the "adjustment to the water and earth" illness and became ill for a week, with temperatures exceeding 103 degrees. A local doctor prescribed some white powdery medication. It apparently worked, and the fever was tamed in two days. I became very weak for at least another ten days after recovery from the fever. I was about to enter college but had never worn a wristwatch and was longing for one. I walked along the Wu-Chong Street in downtown Taipei, where most of the big jewelry stores were located. I was fond of those ultrathin watches. I told Mama about going to find a tutoring job to make some money to buy a watch after I got home.

"Mama, I found a watch in a store today. It is so thin and very pretty. I am going to find a tutoring job to pay for it," I said.

"Nonsense. If you need a watch, Baba will get you one. I will tell him to figure out a way to get you a watch," she said with a mysterious expression.

When Baba came home that night, Mama told him about my desire to buy a wristwatch.

"Oh! That's easy. I will just write a paper. The fee advanced to me should be enough for a good watch," he told me. In the next four nights, Baba wrote papers until past midnight. A month later, Baba gave me NT$400 to buy a watch. I bought the thinnest wristwatch on the market for NT$320. I appreciated Baba's sacrifices in taking four nights to work for my watch and his ability to write articles that were readily accepted by well-known publishers.

In the local newspaper, I read an announcement about a college program that was a United States university-sponsored degree program for engineering education, offered by the Taiwan Normal College. Graduates of the program would be sent to the United States for graduate studies paid by the program. That announcement was so powerful that it shocked the whole island because going to school in the United States was next to impossible for any common folks in Taiwan. Only the very rich and children of a few high-ranking officials could think of going to school in the United States. As a result, applicants swamped the admissions office of the college.

I already had my mind made up to enter an engineering program in another university before this announcement. I was still not convinced that this was the school I wanted to attend, although the offer was most attractive. Almost all my classmates who graduated from Kao-Shiung Provincial High School had applied for admission. I also filled out an application just to gain some experience in entrance examinations. I didn't think I had any chance to be admitted because there were over 2,000 people registered to take examinations, including many people who were already enrolled in other prestigious colleges.

The examination was scheduled for three days. Each day had two subjects. I never had time to do any preparation but thought I did fine in most of the subjects. Since there were so many top students in this contest, I figured my chance of beating them in test scores was very small.

A week after the examination, the result was posted on the college's bulletin board. I was reluctant to go there but Yao-Hwa urged me to go. He was more anxious than I was.

"Let's go and see the bulletin. Maybe you are on it." He rushed me.

"I don't think I have a chance. There are so many good students who took the test. Besides, I want to attend a school with electrical engineering." I was still not willing to ride the bike fifteen minutes to the college.

"Maybe some of your classmates have made it. Aren't you curious about them?"

"All right, I will go, but I want you to know that I wouldn't be disappointed if I am not making it," I said. I was just not anxious to be accepted into the program.

When we arrived at the big board, a big crowd of more than two hundred people were there reading the baseball-size letters of names. There were fifty people selected plus ten backup candidates pending physical examinations of the fifty selected.

"Your name is on it!" Yao-Hwa screamed.

I read it from twenty feet away and saw my name ranked eleventh on the bulletin.

"I still don't believe it, but I am happy. Now I must decide what to do," I said.

"That is a god headache. Isn't it?" Yao-Hwa said smiling.

"Not necessarily. Now I think hard about what to do next. Let's go home now," I said. I grabbed him away from the crowd.

I was among the original fifty selected students. I was happy to be selected but was not excited about it because I had other plans. From my graduating class of about 120 students from Kao-Shiung, I was the only one who passed the entrance examinations. Of the ten backup candidates, only three were not selected. Two of them later became internationally known scholars—one in mathematics and the other in international law.

The college would pay all tuition, expenses, uniforms, and a stipend for the entire four-year degree program. Seven backup candidates were accepted to the program, which meant seven out of the original fifty were found to have tuberculosis. Although I did not know, there was a shadow on my left lung that was the calcified TB. The doctor told me it was considered cured and was not a health threat when the TB-infected area was calcified. Although I was accepted, I was reluctant to enroll in the program because I wanted to be an electrical engineer instead of teaching in technical schools, as the program was intended. I went and sought advice from my old friends.

"Jian-Hsiu, I am unfortunately being accepted, because I have my mind made up for another school," I told my high school buddy who was in Taipei at that time.

"Well, you just don't accept the admission and give another backup candidate a chance," he said.

"But I am attracted by the offer to send me to the United States after graduation. If I don't take this offer now, I may never afford to go to the United States for graduate studies." I couldn't make up my mind.

"If I were you, I would take the offer now. It's a once-in-a-lifetime opportunity," he told me.

"All right, that helps. Thanks for the advice. I will still think about it."

When I talked to Baba about my concerns, Baba was upset that I even hesitated about this great opportunity to receive free college education and the opportunity to go to the United States.

"You need to think very carefully. Where do you find the money to pay for tuition, room, and board if you are going to Taiwan University?" Baba fumed.

"Well, I can tutor and find other work to pay for the cost," I said.

"But how can you be sure you will be able to make enough money to pay for all that?"

"I just don't want to be a high school or a technical schoolteacher. I want to be an electrical engineer," I insisted.

"You can always switch your major after the first degree. You are so young, and there is plenty of time for you to get a second or third degree. I advise you to accept this rare offer soon." Baba was not happy with my resistance to enter the Normal College.

"I will give your advice a serious consideration," I said.

"Consideration? You just do as I said!" Baba exploded.

"Yes. Baba, I will." I said it just to calm him down a little.

After considering the cost of going to the other university I wanted to attend, the offer to study in the United States graduate program, and the stipend and the four-year free education, did move me quite a bit toward accepting the offer. After all, this was only in January. I had six months to change my mind and to change the school, so I decided to enter the Normal College.

I began my college life at the age of eighteen, an age typical to students entering a college in Taiwan. The freshman program started with orientation led by upperclassmen. It was mandatory to live in the dormitory for the first six months. The three meals were very good from the local living standard. I shared the bunker in the dorm room with three other classmates. I thought the regiment of living in the dorm was like in a military boot camp that reminded me a lot about the camps I had been in years ago.

In the freshmen classroom, each student was assigned a permanent seat, same as I had experienced in grade school and high school. There was no elective class for that entire year, and everyone was supposed to sit in the same seat throughout the two semesters. I was assigned a seat in the front row just by chance. Among the fifty students enrolled, only eleven were girls. The curriculum was the standard engineering freshman type with basic mathematics and sciences courses. I thought the college professors were quite good, but no one was as impressive as my senior physics teacher in high school. My classmates mostly were my age group, but there were over twenty and one was just sixteen.

There was this heavyset fellow, Mai-Tai Yang, who had a round, smiling face and looked nice enough but was very loud in any crowd and was a show-off enthusiast. Above all, he was an egocentric exhibitionist. As I was just recovering from an illness and looked pale and weak, Mai-Tai thought that was a great opportunity for him to show off his strength or power. During a lunch break in the first week, just before the afternoon class started, I was sitting in the first row and minding my own business. For no reason whatsoever, Mai-Tai started raising hell in front of the girls by picking on me.

"Hey, you. You do not look good at all. Look at me. I am talking to you. Are you scared of me?" he yelled as he put his fists on my desk.

"I am not scared of you just because you have a big fat face," I responded.

"Hey! Do you want to make trouble with me? Do you know who are you talking to? You little chicken shit!" he shouted.

"No. I don't want to get in trouble with you. I don't know you," I said.

"I say you are a coward. I can put you down with just one punch!" he shouted as he made a mean gesture, waving his big fists in front of my face.

"You look to me nothing but a big potbelly, no-good slop with a big mouth to go with it," I said angrily.

Mai-Tai became very upset, since he did not gain any upper hand in the exchange.

"You want to arm wrestle me? You coward." He was aggressive.

Now he wanted to show off his strength in front of the whole class, especially the girls. I knew he had picked the wrong guy to wrestle with and what a dumb mistake he was making! I knew I could easily beat him without any effort, but how could he know just by looking at me! I first tried to put it off and told him, "Look, Mai-Tai. I am in no mood to wrestle with you today. How about let us try it tomorrow?"

"I know you are a chicken. What's wrong to do it now?" He raised his voice.

"Can we do it after the class? I really don't like to do it in front of so many people."

He became more aggressive, since from his judgment I was feared of him and of showing my weakness.

"You are a coward. I have all of the witnesses here to prove it!" he shouted.

"All right, you asked for it." That was too much for me to take so I agreed to wrestle him right away.

Some good-hearted classmates came over and tried to save my grace by trying to talk Mai-Tai out of it. "Hey! Mai-Tai, you are so much bigger than Tien-Ren. We know you are stronger than him. Why don't you just leave him alone?" someone in the back said.

Of course, Mai-Tai did not agree to that. He could not wait to see people cheering at him and calling him a hero. We rolled up our sleeves. His arm was almost twice as big as mine, but I knew most of it was just a bundle of fluffy fat. We started wrestle on the teacher's desk. People just piled on each other to watch us. I knew many of them were feeling sorry for me. I teased him a bit by letting him push my arm down just a few degrees. He thought he could declare the victory at any moment, but that was as far as I would allow him to bend my arm. When he could not put me down right away, he was really exhausted by his lack of training. After about five minutes standing still, he was psychologically defeated, because he was supposed to nail me in a few seconds.

I easily slammed his arm hard on the desk. Everybody was surprised and astonished by the outcome. Mai-Tai was totally shocked, embarrassed, and swore up and down to save his face. "You are only a dumb ox! You just have muscles but no brains!" he shouted.

"All right, Mai-Tai, you won," I said. Everybody in the classroom laughed. From that day on, Mai-Tai avoided making any trouble to me.

Our youngest classmate, at sixteen, Gio-Hwa Wang, was a very nice, gentle soul. He came from a wealthy family and had more pocket money than most of the other classmates. Mai-Tai borrowed money from Gio-Hwa constantly and Gio-Hwa always obliged. I imagined all the money he borrowed was for his taste buds. Everybody knew about what went on, but Mai-Tai did not care about what others might say about him as long he could reach his goal. In a few months, Mai-Tai had accumulated a significant amount of debt from Gio-Hwa. When Mai-Tai got paid by the school or received some money from home, he would have some money in front a group of classmates and announce, "Gio-Hwa, I am paying back the money to you now, all right? But since you really do not know what to do with the money, let me help you to buy some food for everyone in our dorm here." He then waved the handful of bills in front of the bunch in the dorm.

Without any approval from Gio-Hwa, Mai-Tai went out and bought a delicacy for himself and brought back some to be shared with others. To Mai-Tai, the money was paid back but Gio-Hwa never saw a penny of his money back. At this point, we gave Mai-Tai a rather unflattering nickname: the turtle egg, which was the equivalent meaning of the SOB or worse. But Mai-Tai did not mind, if he could take advantage of others. Even with all his shortcomings, Mai-Tai really was a good-hearted fellow. He never intended to inflict any harm to others and just wanted to satisfy his big ego in front of a crowd. In addition, he was a very good student and a good basketball player, but we never became friends. He left the college six months later and transferred to a more prestigious university.

After the first semester, I commuted from home to school every day as most other students did. In the winter season, at five o'clock, the street was in total darkness except for the dim lights from the few dim bulbs on the light poles. Accordingly, all the bikes had to be equipped with headlights or the rider could carry a flashlight. I often forgot such matters when I started school in the bright early morning.

"Hey, you get off your bike and come with me," a burly policeman barked, shining his flashlight right in my eyes. I recognized he was Sergeant Lu, who had caught me for the same reason last week.

"What's wrong, Officer?" I asked as I stopped right in front of him, knowing exactly what the matter was.

"It's you again! You must come with me to see Lieutenant Liang again. I don't think you can get away this time." He waved at me with his flashlight to follow him to the Seventh Precinct nearby.

"It is you again! Ha! You have never learned, have you?" Lieutenant Liang barked at me while he sat in his chair behind the big desk. He was a thirty some, lanky, tall fellow with heavy glasses on his nose but few hairs on his head.

"Lieutenant Liang, you caught me again. I forgot my flashlight because when I left home it was very bright in the morning. When I left the school just now, I didn't know where to find a flashlight at this time. You guys are here to protect us from bike accidents in the darkness. I really appreciate that. But you have caused so much inconvenience for me and wasting a lot of your time just to fine me one yuan. Or you can put me in you jail for the night, so I can get a free meal." I was in a mood to argue with him.

"I hate fast talkers. Why don't you just take you bike and get out of here? And don't let me see you again," he said loudly but not in anger.

"Thank you, Lieutenant Liang. I am leaving." And I got out there as fast as I could. I hoped that was the last time the lieutenant would see me behind his desk.

Before the end of the second semester of the first year, Professor Hoole and Dr. Noble of the Pennsylvania State University came to Taiwan to coordinate this joint education program. It turned out our education program was set up totally wrong. This program was intended to educate industrial arts teachers and not engineering teachers as was advertised in the papers. The first-year curriculum had been set up as the traditional engineering curriculum with standard divisions of electrical engineering, mechanical engineering, civil engineering, and chemical engineering. According to the Penn State plan, the program had to be completely overhauled.

This change of program had caused a full-scale rebellion of the entire class and the second group of another fifty students. Both groups of students were strictly selected through very rigorous examinations. The two classes were the cream of the crop of high school graduates and some students had previously enrolled in other colleges. This change took us all by surprise and we did not want the changes, but because it was dictated by Penn State University, the college had to do exactly as they said. To us students, that just did not make any sense and we felt deceived or betrayed.

We organized a group of ten students to represent the two classes that totaled one hundred students. I was among the ten representatives. We outlined the strategy and talking paper. The key point was that the college had misled the public in that newspaper announcement. We went to the department chairman, the dean of the school, the president of the college, director of the Taiwan Education Department, and finally, the minister of education of the Republic of China. The group met with each of the officials individually. We also called a press conference and invited education heads to answer questions. Schoolwork was left unattended because this was the key issue we had to resolve before any study was meaningful to us. The ten of us were constantly out of the school, running back and forth between the school and offices of those important people that made decisions for our lives.

After three months of protests, walkout, and negotiation, we reached an agreement. The agreement was to allow all the students to transfer to the University of Taiwan in Taipei or the Cheng-Kung University in Tainan, the two most prestigious institutions in Taiwan, without taking any examinations. The only exception was that students who wished to transfer to the medical school needed to take examination in biology. Our department chairman, Mr. Po-Yen Koo, interviewed each of the students and tried to convenience us to stay with the current program. The biggest incentive, of course, was the promise of the opportunity to go to the United States for advanced studies. Going to the United States was only the dream of children of the rich and the powerful. To us common folks, it was beyond our dreams. Therefore, the promise of going to the United States, and paid by the program, was the strongest incentive for us to stay.

Of the fifty students in my class, only twenty-one decided to stay and I was one of them. My reasons were that I felt comfortable with the school environment here and had permission from the college of sciences to allow me to take mathematics and physics courses. In the meantime, the college was elevated to a university status. I thought with my preparations in basic mathematics and sciences, I would be able to enter an engineering program later in a graduate program.

CHAPTER 9

A GENIUS

When we moved into this house in Taipei, it is one of the four units in the eight-foot brick wall enclosed apartment. The next day, I spot a boy with a short built and a disproportionally large head. He looked like a smart boy. So, I walked toward him and extended my hand,

"My name in Tien-ren Cheng. What is yours?"

"My name is Yao Hwa Hsiung. Did you just move in? I live in the first unit. Where do you live?" He said.

"I live in the second unit. Right next to yours." I said. That started our long-time friendship.

At that time, I was 18 and he was just 14 years of age. He was very intelligent and mature beyond his age. He could argue all sort matters with me and at times he made feel he was invincible. But he has secrets that were untold to most that knew him.

His father worked for a shipping company. I understood he had held a high-ranking managerial position. I called him Uncle Hsiung. His father was an easy-going guy and easy to get along with. But he rarely stayed home. Yao Hwa, his three sisters stayed with their Mother in this two-bedroom small apartment. We were next door neighbors, so we meet each other every day. We would talk about everything. His mother was a middle age woman, kind, tender and had a good humor. I called her Aunt Hsiung. His three sisters Shio Yun, Shio Yen and Shio Ron. Shio Yun was one year younger than him. The two fight like dogs and cats. Shio Yen and Shio Run were much younger, so I had little impression of them.

"Who should marry Shio Yun is going to having bad luck forever." Yao Hwa would tell me.

"Why are you always going against her. I feel you have too much bias there." I said.

"You don't know only staying with her daily you would know how vicious she is. The heart of a woman is the most poisonous thing." He said.

But I found Shio Yun beautiful and gentle. Due the age difference and her brother's influence, I did not make a lot of contact with her.

A year later we moved to Chen Gong Village a near by military housing compound, belong to Army Central Command. Therefore, Yao Hwa and I still meet frequently. He, at that time, entered high school. One day about half year later, I saw him looking very down.

"Big Head Hsiung what happen to you? You don't look to hot." I said.

"My shameless father has left us." He said.

"Why? It is just temporary. Isn't it?" I am totally surprised.

"Not so. Because he has a new lover. Now he just abandoned us." He said, tear rolled out his eyes.

"This is really unthinkable. Does your mother have any plans? How about your living support?" I asked.

"I really don't know. We will figure something out somehow." He said.

His mother had no working experience, the whole family had lost sources for living. Fortunately, their relatives chipped in in and help. Yao Hwa had to work while going to school. At that time, he was sixteen years old. My father found out about Yao Hwa's situation and was sympathetic to him. My father found him a job within the Army General Headquarters working as a draftsman. He did his job well and encountered no difficulties. When moved out from his home, I put him in the video room of my school to sleep. At night he would eat supper with us. This matter I did not report to the Chairman, Mr. Koo until Yao Hwa found a place to stay.

While he worked, he was attending school at the University High School in the class of Forty-Three. When attending the high school, he was in "love" with a girl. He was talking about the girl to me all day long. The girl's name is Goo Tse Fung (Young Phenix) so he named himself Goo Long (Old Dragon). This would mean dragon and phenix matching each other. The Goo Long was used throughout his lifetime as his pen name. But finally, his one-sided love ended with no results.

Yao Hwa Hsiung had inseparable reputation involving sex. Ever since I knew him, when he was 15 years old, he often mentions about that he had sexual relationship with certain girls. I treated it as a child's boasting and ignored him. But with the increase of age, this matter became more serious.

"I had sex with a girl yesterday. She was some one I bumped in occasionally." One day he told me.

"How can you ruin her so causally. What she is going to do." I was a little angry.

"You are really an old-fashioned guy. This kind of things are happening everywhere and every day." I was speechless. In the days to come, this king of things happened too often, people were saying things behind him.

Upon graduation from high school he entered Dang Chiang University. Whether he had completed his degree, I don't know. But he had gained and the fame for being a novel writer regardless he graduates or not from the University.

Yao Hwa was a famous writer while he was a student in the University. He had a vast reader and fan group. His books were mostly Kung Fu and ancient Chinese romance. Since his novel related to ancient Chinese history, so he took his scripts to my father for him to review.

"Uncle Cheng please review my writing. Any correction is appreciated." He would ask my father.

My father really read his novel carefully,

"Your writing is not bad. But the facts of history you have not been very careful. You still have much to learn." My father told him.

"Thank you, Uncle Cheng. I will study harder. Next time I will show you a much better one."

But from what I know he has did come to see my father several times.

"Dad what do you think Yao Hwa's writing?"

"He is so young and can write so well is not bad. I think he is a genius in writing." My father said. He never praised anyone so highly.

Later I went to the U.S.A. from news articles and from people who knew him, his movie "Tsu Lue Shiung" was popular in Taiwan, Hong Kong and the Mainland, His Kung Fu novel and movie were numerous, and all were very popular. In 1978, I return to Taipei. Think of Yao Hwa, so I call him. The answerer was a female,

"Hello, May I ask whom you call?"

"I am old friend with Yao Hwa Hsiung, May I speak to him."

A few seconds later. The girl asked,

"May I know your name?"

"My name is Tien-Ren Cheng." I said.

With in seconds, there was excited voice,

"Tien-Ren Cheng, Old pal, Is that really you?" I was not familiar with that voice, but I know who it was.

"Big head Hsiung long time no see, how are you?"

"I am fine. Where are you?" He asked.

"I am in Taipei, my parents' house."

"OK. Don't move. I will pick you up at five pm." He said.

"OK. I will be waiting for you,"

That afternoon he came at five sharps. He visited my parents.

"Uncle and Aunt Cheng, how are you?" He said to my parents.

My parents were equally happy to see him. They had heard his success news from the news stations.

After a brief saying hello, he told me,

"I have to take you to see some of my friends."

I follow him out of my parents' house and entered his fancy automobile. It was a stretched Limo. He briefly talked to the driver and the driver was driving the can away. After seventeen years, Taipei had changed a lot, to the degree that I didn't know where I was.

"Where are we going?" I asked.

"When we arrive there, you would know." Yao Hwa said.

Soon we arrived at a luxury hotel. Two middle aged men came out, both are well dressed. They shook hand with Yao Hwa than Yao Hwa introduce them to me. Now I had forgotten their names. Then we walked into a large meeting room. Where sat about fifteen people. All well dressed and all looked like tycoons, they all stand up when we entered. Yao Hwa sat at the head seat while I was seated next to him. He pointed to his right-hand side and said.

"This is XXX, a big screen writer. This is XXX a big movie star,..." He introduced to all guests. And then he started speech, "Thank you, you all at my short invitation to come to this meeting. Today I want to introduce to you my big brother Tien-Ren Cheng, whom I have mentioned to many of you in the past. When I was down and no where to go. This brother provided me with living space. When I was no means to provide for mu self. This brother helps me find a job." At this time, he choked, and tears came down his cheeks. Never thought he was so sentimental, and these things had happened so long ago.

"Today Tien-Ren Cheng, my big brother is a successful college professor in the United States of America. Please let me use my sincerest heart to welcome this person..."

He was very excited. When spoke he often had broken down into tears. After the fancy dinner he used him limo to take home and said goodbye to me.

The day after I left Taipei and returned America. Yao Hwa and I were busy bodies, so we did not communicate to each other. Time goes by fast, a few years later, I saw on the news Yao Hwa had died of over drinking. He was forty-eight years old. His friend put forty-eight bottles of XO in his gasket for memorial.

CHAPTER 10

RIOTING AGAINST THE AMERICANS

Our American-funded program was the richest in the entire island nation. We had a brand-new building for the new program, new audiovisual equipment, and several best-equipped laboratories and shops. All of which were paid through the USAID program. Because of my electronics technical experience in the past, I was put in charge of planning and ordering equipment for the electronics laboratory and the electrical shop when I was just a sophomore. I had a lot of fun designing the laboratory's layout and selected equipment from catalogs provided by US companies. After I submitted the proposals, the university administration immediately ordered them. All equipment arrived from American factories in a matter of two to three months. I was amazed by the workmanship of the products, the promptness of shipping, and the thoroughness in packaging.

Looking at the craftsmanship and the fine details in every aspect of the equipment and hand tools, my beliefs and respects to those people who made these wonderful tools of human achievement in technology were solidly enhanced. I had heard so much about America, but this was the first time I had been intimately engaged to those people half a world away through their technological work. I had been amazed by those broken aircraft parts I picked up from the crash sites; the new equipment just knocked me off my feet. What kind of people and what kind of working environment they had to be able to make things like that! I'd really like to go there to meet those people and learn from them, and in the program here, I should be heading that way. I couldn't wait for the day to come that I could really go to America. Well, at least I could daydream about it.

The chairman appointed me to set up the laboratories and the shops with a group of hired technicians. I was most excited about the assignments and did it free of charge. In addition to taking courses in my major field, I also took many courses in physics and mathematics. With the added busy work of setting up the facilities, I had very little time to play basketball, soccer, and other extracurricular activities.

To take courses from other department was not a simple matter. I did not know if it was school politics or what. The chairman of the physics department, Dr. Ko-Chun Chen, was unwilling to accept a student from another department to take courses in his department for reasons of limited seating, quality control, and maintenance of the prestige of the physics department. After he reviewed my transcripts and the recommendation by Mr. Koo, he conditionally allowed me to register for courses in the physics department. The condition was to maintain a B or better average to continue and to be evaluated at the end of each semester. I agreed to all the terms.

"Tien-Ren, I have promised him that you will do well in his department. I hope you will set an example for others in our department," Mr. Koo told me. I knew if I should fail in physics courses, no one else from our department could get permission to take any course there in the future. I took the promise to Mr. Koo seriously. Although the courses I took in the physics department were much tougher than any course in the industrial education department, I did not feel the burden of carrying the full load in both departments. Since I had to do well in the physics department, I spent twice as much time to study for those physics courses as for my major courses. The first report card was not a surprise to me; I had all A grades from the physics courses and only on A- grades from my major courses. Mr. Koo was pleased because I did not let him down. Two or three fellow students from my department could take physics courses without any objections from the physics department head, at later times.

In an early fall afternoon, I was in a classroom trying to solve some problems from my physics class. A big commotion was going in the main hallway. I went out of the classroom.

"What is going on here? You guys are so excited," I said to a fellow student.

"I am not excited. I am mad as hell," he fumed.

"Why?" I was confused.

"Haven't you heard the news about the American sergeant who has killed a Taiwanese gangster when they argued about how to divide the drug proceeds?" He was a bit annoyed that I was in the dark.

"Yes, I did see that in the newspaper a month ago. They are both bad guys, but why are you so upset about it?" I questioned.

"Well, haven't you heard the latest news?"

"No, tell me about it," I said.

"The American sergeant had a hearing in the US military court and was freed for no wrongdoing. The American soldier had killed an unarmed Taiwanese citizen, and they say he did nothing wrong!" He was hopping mad.

"Slow down. You mean the American soldier was let go just like that, not even a day in jail?" My admiration of American people suddenly diminished.

"The Americans are really no good. They have no concept of justice. They are not treating us as people. Then can't just let the murderer of our citizen go free without any punishment," another student said, waving his hand up and down. He apparently was extremely upset.

"You are so right. If someone kicks my dog, he shows his disregard to me. This is ridiculous! I don't care how much aid the Americans given us. I'd rather throw the money back to them and have them get out of here!" someone shouted excitingly.

All the students listening to him became very emotional about this injustice. I could not believe the Americans were so stupid.

Didn't they understand people's feelings? Or were they so arrogant that they didn't care what we felt? I was extremely disappointed to the whole situation. I wished I had nothing to do with the American program at the university.

"Let's go and protest against the US Embassy!" someone in the crowd shouted.

This group of about fifty students, including me, stormed out of the school building and was joined by two or three large groups of students on the way to the US Embassy a few miles away.

"Down with the Americans!" the group chanted under direction of a fellow using a megaphone.

"Americans go home!" they shouted.

"Yankees go home! We don't want your dirty aid! Go home!" another group shouted.

Emotions ran high and the chanting was from deep in our hearts. We really hated the Americans. How could we love someone who handed us a bundle of money and then spit on our faces? We'd rather died of starvation or be killed in a war against the Communists with dignity than be humiliated like this.

It took this noisy group thirty minutes by fast walking to reach the US Embassy in northern Taipei. There were already thousands of people gathering in front of the white brick building. The normally opened iron gate was shut tight and was locked up. The Taiwanese police force was guarding the embassy with weapons in hand. More and more people joined in; the streets around the embassy soon were filled with protesters. Most of the protesters were college age and some of them looked like high school students.

The protesters were disorganized without a leader but soon someone in the crowd with a megaphone started to lead the chanting.

"Down with the US injustice! Americans go home!" they shouted.

Soon some hot heads started throwing rocks at the building. A sequence of the glass-breaking noise was heard above the chanting. The police tried to push the protesters back and the mood began to turn ugly toward the police.

"Why are you protecting the ugly Americans?" someone shouted.

A few rocks were aimed at the policemen. Suddenly, there was huge smoke and fire bursting near the gate and a second fire nearby was started. I could not see it from where I was, but the noise and the smell told me that some cars were set on fire. Since very few people in Taiwan had cars at that time, I assumed the cars all belonged to the US Embassy.

"The gas in the cars is going to explode! Get away from the cars!" someone shouted.

I could see the wave of people push its way away from the flames.

Not more than a minute later, I heard two or three loud explosions and saw the surge of flames in the direction of the burning cars. The police force was not large enough to hold back the angry crowd. A few students climbed over the iron gate, climbed up the flagpole inside the eight-foot wall, and pulled down the US flag. A student produced a bottle of gasoline, poured it on the flag, and set it on fire. Just as the crowd about to push down the iron gate, several truckloads of heavily armed soldiers arrived at the scene. They were in full riot gear and started ordering people to disperse. At that point, my schoolmates knew that if we stayed here any longer, someone would get hurt. We all walked away from the scene and returned to the school. I heard from the radio later that the crowd did disperse quickly, and no one was injured.

The whole international incident was totally avoidable, if the American officials in Taipei were handling the situation with a bit of common sense and were not so arrogant about it. It was a Taiwanese drug smuggler who collaborated with a US Army sergeant to smuggle dope into Taiwan. When they had differences in splitting the loot, the sergeant pulled a gun and killed the Taiwanese gangster. That was in the news, and because that was a fight between two criminals, no one had paid much attention to it. Since the gangster did not have a weapon in his possession, it was apparently a homicide. If the US military court just sentenced the sergeant to some jail time for killing a person, even if it was just for a short term, it would be acceptable to Taiwanese people, at least to me. After the riot, the US government formally apologized to Taiwanese people, court-martialed, and sentenced the sergeant to jail for a few years.

I thought this unfortunate international incident was due to poorly trained US personnel overseas. Many military and civil service people sent overseas by the US government were not properly trained. Some of them were outright arrogant and lacked sensitivity. This was not the only incident that was hurting the American image overseas. There had to be more such events like the Taiwan incident, such as the one depicted in the movie *The Ugly Americans*. But deep in our heart, we knew it was a name undeserving by Americans. It was just the mishandling of sensitive cases by a few undertrained and less selective US personnel.

"I know the great majority of Americans are not like the official in the embassy. You know I lived in Chicago for five years before I returned here to teach," Professor Tai, one of our senior faculties in the department, told me one day after class.

"Professor Tai, why don't they send some smarter people to represent the country instead of those idiots?" I asked.

"Well, they may have a different selection process based on criteria, not how to make friends or represent a good image of America. I don't know the real criteria, but I would venture to say the spy skills are more important for them," he said.

"But we are one of their allies in Asia. Why do they want to spy on us?" I was confused by his statement.

"It is very complex. As far as I know, all embassies are spy nests, regardless of it is friend or foe. Still, I am telling you the American people are not like what the officials in the embassy had represented. I have many friends in America. They would be embarrassed by this incident if they knew about it."

"Thank you, Professor Tai. I was so disappointed with the Americans, I almost thought about quitting this program. Now I will stay and go to America after graduation and see for myself," I said.

"I am sure you will not be disappointed in America when you go there," Professor Tai told me.

His talk and my own careful analysis of the incident had restored my confidence that I had made a correct choice and still admired the home of technological wonders.

CHAPTER 11

THE YOUNG ENTREPRENEURS

"One needs enough money to make a living, but too much money will corrupt one's life," Mama told me many times as I grew up in war-torn China. I thought I understood perfectly what she had meant, but after I had grown up, the questions of what is "enough" and what is "too much" were blurred since no one I had known suffered from too much money. The schoolteachers and texts always told us, "Do not seek wealth but seek greatness in what you do." To make money had never entered my mind in the past nineteen years. Now that I had done quite a lot of free work for people and schools, was it fair to accept compensation? I decided the answer was a resounding affirmative.

One day in my junior year, Mr. Koo called me into his office. With him was a middle-aged lady. Mr. Koo introduced her to me. "Tien-Ren, this is Mrs. Li, the deputy minister of education. And this is Tien-Ren Cheng, the electronics wizard I have talked to you about."

"Mrs. Li, this is indeed an honor meeting you in person," I said.

The Island Heaven

"It is very nice to meet you. I have heard a lot about you. That's why I am here today." Mrs. Li quickly got to the point. "The ministry has received a large quantity of electronics equipment from the repatriation of war by the Japanese government. I need someone to identify the equipment. We want to distribute the equipment among colleges who need it. Are you willing to work as a consultant for the ministry?"

I was always intrigued by electronic gears and was curious about unknowns. I thought, *Wow! A consultant to the ministry!*

"It would be my honor to have your trust in me with the responsibility. I will do my best to get the job done. When do I start?"

"I would like to see the work starting right away. I will have the ministry staff contact you tomorrow and arrange your transportation to the warehouse near the ministry. Is it convenient for you?" Mrs. Li asked.

"I will be ready to see the equipment tomorrow at any time," I said.

"I will have my aide call the department office here later this afternoon," she said.

"Thank you, Mrs. Li," I said. "Dr. Koo, would you have your secretary notify me when the ministry calls?"

"Certainly, I will make sure you get the message as soon as it comes in," Dr. Koo said with a broad smile.

"Good-bye, Mrs. Li!" I excused myself from the office.

Later I found out that the ministry had received a warehouse full of World War II military and laboratory electronic equipment from Japan. The ministry had difficulties to find someone who could identify the equipment.

At the age of 22 Graduate from College

They needed to identify and distribute this equipment to laboratories at various universities and colleges quickly.

Mrs. Li's aide called and left a message saying they would pick me up at eight thirty the next morning in front of the department building. The warehouse was about a forty-minute bike ride from the university, but the ministry would send staff and a car to take me to the warehouse.

The next morning, the ministry staff member, Guo-Si Huang, came with a sedan to take me to the warehouse. In the giant warehouse, I saw piles upon piles of wooden crates and large antenna structures.

"How many people do you have working in the warehouse?" I asked the warehouse staff.

"Just the custodian and two movers," he replied.

I took some notes and asked Mr. Huang to take me back to the university. I went to see Mr. Koo for advice.

"Mr. Koo, it is going to be a very big job at the ministry warehouse. I need to recruit some of my classmates to assist me, and I think we need to be compensated for the work we are doing. Do you agree?"

"Yes, not only I agree but I encourage you to have the entrepreneurial ideas. I will call Mrs. Li and ask her to take it into consideration," he said.

"Well, we will do the job even the ministry is not paying us, but it would be nice for us to earn some spending money," I said.

"I am sure they have the budget, even if you don't ask them. They will compensate you after the work is done, but I think it is better to have a firm understanding in the beginning," he said. "Just leave this to me. I will see it done."

I recruited two classmates as my assistants. Shi-Chun Yen and Jin-Hwan Chen both were well versed with electronics. They were happy to have this opportunity to work on a project of such magnitude. The day we were to begin our work, Mrs. Li's aide, Mr. Huang, told me that the ministry had agreed to pay us a lump sum consulting fee when we completed the work. I was thrilled about the income, since I had not earned any money from work in my whole life. Although Mr. Huang did not tell me how much it would be, from my point of view, I would be satisfied with any amount the ministry would pay.

"Ay! Fellows, the ministry will pay us for the equipment identification work," I said. "But I don't know how much they will pay us. In any event, we will divide that into three equal shares."

"I really did not expect to be paid at all. This is sure a surprise," Jin-Hwan said.

"That is great! I need the money to buy a new harmonica," Shi-Chun said. "I don't know about you two, but this would be my first job that will actually pay me money for my work."

"Me too. I got my spending money from my parents before attending the college. I have never received any payment for work either," Jin-Hwan said.

"Well, me neither. The only money we have received was from the school and our parents. We are adults now. It's time for us to make some money on our own," I said.

The next day after school, the three of us rode the bikes to the warehouse, where three workers were ready to help us. I devised a system for the three of us working on three different piles. The custodians would take the crates from the top and place them on the floor first. They also helped to open the crate with heavy tools. The three of us would act individually, taking the equipment out from the crates for identifications and writing down specifications. For me, it was like opening surprise gift boxes with great curiosity and enthusiasm. When the two fellows had found something new, they would ask me for consultation or to share the excitement.

"Look what have I found here!" Shi-Chun exclaimed one morning. Both Jin-Hwan and I rushed over to see what discovered. It was a typical Japanese military, yellowish-brown, metal box and measured eighteen inches wide, twenty inches tall, and about twelve inches thick. On the front face, it was full of dials and other indicators and was clearly marked as "direction finder" in kanji (Chinese characters).

"It is an ordinary directional finder. What's so exciting about it?" I asked.

"Well, I have seen them in the movies but not an actual unit. I wish we could take it to the school and play with it." Shi-Chun was always very playful.

"No, I am afraid not. We are hired to work here. I don't think the ministry will allow us to take anything for our school," I said.

"Can we just borrow it for a few days? Maybe?" He wouldn't give up.

"All right, I will ask Mr. Huang, but don't bet he will agree," I said.

"That would be great if he agrees," Shi-Chun said.

That late afternoon when Mr. Huang came to the warehouse to see the work in progress, I asked him, "Mr. Huang, we are very much interested in looking closely with that directional finder. Can we take it to our lab and study it for a few days?"

"By all means. If you fellows can really use it, I will ask the minister to allocate it to your school," he said.

"No, Mr. Huang, that is not necessary. We will just borrow it for three days, but I thank you just the same," I said.

"Why in the world did you turn down his offer to let us keep it?" Shi-Chun was upset with me.

"Look. The directional finder is nothing but a radio receiver. You need two of them to detect the position of a transmitter. This thing standing alone is useless. If we are going to get anything for our school, it must come from the professors, not us." I had to be firm with my buddies.

In the process, we found quantities of new and used radars, direction finders, radio transmitter\receivers, sonar systems, oscilloscopes, signal generators, waveform generators, antennas, vacuum tubes, and passive parts. We separated them, wrote specifications, described their potential applications, and cataloged them. I wished we had more time to turn on the power and test the equipment—it would really be interesting—but there was not enough time to do any testing at all. There were just too many items to identify and to specify.

We went to work in the warehouse every afternoon after classes. The ministry officials gave banquets for the three of us each

Saturday night. There would be five or six of the ministry officials accompanying us at the banquets and the expenses were paid from the project budget. The entire job was completed in five months. We made the identification and specifications of all major equipment. We also wrote the general application for each of the equipment: a four-volume, inch-thick report. Officials from the ministry distributed the equipment to needy colleges. My university did receive several pieces of the electronics equipment; all went to the college of sciences.

At the end of the work, Mrs. Li hosted a banquet, inviting Mr. Koo and other VIPs to thank the three students. A gift box and an envelope were given to each of us. After the banquet, the three of us opened the boxes and found pen sets and a dictionary. In the fat envelope, we found a stack of cash exceeding a whole year's stipend at the college. It was a large and generous sum for a college student. As I requested, the three of us received the same amount of compensation. We were all very happy.

During the junior year in the college, I had never sought the position, but I was elected president of the class. Reluctantly, I accepted it. Again, I thought with the talent we had among the classmates, we should be able to practice our learned skills and work to earn money. I strongly believed that what we had learned at home and in schools about "being poor is honorable" was totally illogical and deadly wrong. To earn money with our ability and effort legally would be truly honorable. As the class president, I thought I would try to market our skills to people needing the expertise.

During the school year, I went to government agencies and private companies to talk to people who might need our help. The response was quite positive. I arranged various consulting jobs for many classmates in my class. From the work done, we gained a wealth of experience in designing and constructing a variety of small projects for the city and some commercial entities. We also had a lot of fun working together, besides making a substantial amount of spending money for all of us. I guessed that was why my classmates reelected me as the president in the senior year. That was the time we had to get serious in finishing the degree requirements and start looking for jobs before graduation. Like all things in real life, experience was very important to new graduates. I believed that the experience we had obtained as consultants would help us as well in job hunting after graduation.

I thought it would be a good idea to get the whole class involved full time in a summer job. My first thought was to call the deputy minister of education, Mrs. Li. She immediately granted me a meeting to see her. I told her about my ideas and told her about the talents we had in the class.

"We are just in the process of establishing a training center for teachers to learn new technology and use new audiovisual equipment for teaching. It is a big job. Do you think you and your classmates can handle that in the summer?" she asked me.

"We have the knowledge of the equipment involved in the project and we have the background in designs. I am confident that we will do a good job on time. I need to have all twenty-one people working on this project. I believe we will have it done in three months or less," I replied without any hesitation.

"Twenty-one people should be sufficient to do the job. I will pay each of you a fixed fee of NT$1,500 per person for the summer job, if you accept this offer. You can start right after the end of the spring semester," Mrs. Li said.

"Thank you for the most generous offer. We will report to work right after the final examination," I replied.

I figured that no one could earn NT$500 a month in the summer, so they should be happy that I agreed to take the job. NT$500 was a month's salary for a full-time junior engineer. I was right. No one in my class complained about the pay.

"I don't believe the ministry is paying us so much money for such simple work, but I am not complaining at all," Sung-Ting, a top-ranked classmate, commented.

"Well, she knows we will deliver good results to her. The money seems big for us, but to the ministry it's peanuts," Kwan-Yen Yang said.

"I think it is important that we do a good job. You see, we are under the supervision of the ministry. It can dictate our future employment," Chen-Bin Chou said. He was always very serious and a deep thinker. He was quite right about it.

That project was to convert an existing building into a fully automated modern demonstration and training complex for high school teachers throughout Taiwan. All my twenty classmates signed up for the work and worked with more than twenty building-renovation workers. The old, brick, two-story building was used as offices by the Japanese. After being taken over by the government of ROC in 1946, it was used for storage of documents and furniture. While the renovation crew was working on the exterior walls and the roof, we worked on the interior floor plans. By the time we finished the drawings, the crew immediately followed our design to renovate the interior. Within three weeks, the interior was completely renovated and painted. We then started to work on the equipment part of the job.

We were at the site around seven thirty in the morning, eating from our lunch bags, and would not leave until eight or nine at night. It was not just hard work only; we also had a lot of fun and a sense of accomplishment when a task was done. The girls were working on art design and drafting, and the boys did all the heavy-duty lifting, cutting, wiring, and electronics testing. Everyone was serious about their assignment. I doubled as the foreman of the group, so I had to do a lot of paperwork after each task was completed.

The work was completed within the three-month time as promised to Mrs. Li. She gave us a big banquet at the end of the project after the ministry had accepted the work. All twenty-one students received a gift box and a fat envelope as expected.

Four years of college life went by fast. Soon we were either looking for a job or waiting for offers from certain schools. Many of my classmates found teaching positions in two-year colleges, vocational schools, or high schools. I did not look for a job elsewhere because I was sure that the department would want to keep me around in the university, but it was not as simple as I thought.

Without any notion in school politics, I assumed the chairman could just hire me, but it was not so. Among the professors and the administrators, a tangle of politics was played on all levels of offices in the university. An intense war among the senior professors in the department to appoint their favorite students to a teaching position in the university had been going on way before we graduated. Then there were people in high places who wanted to do favors to people who wanted to become college faculty. Traditionally, a department would keep the highest-ranking graduates to stay with the department to teach. Since our department was new and small, there were only three openings in the department and more than six senior professors had their choices and recommendations. The two graduates that ranked number 1 and 2 were selected without any question. I was ranked number 5 in the class with my overall average. My major field grades were not as high as my grades in physics and mathematics departments. My professor in electronics who wanted to keep me fought with other professors in meetings after meetings with the chairman. It was a weeklong struggle in meetings among the chairman and those six professors. Finally, they voted for special skills and not just grade averages. I easily won the points and was appointed to a position in the university as a teaching assistant. I was very happy for the decision, but I knew that they really needed someone to teach electronics classes immediately, not just serve as a teaching assistant to a professor like the other did.

In January 1957, I started my teaching career at the university as a teaching assistant at twenty-two years old. Normally, a teaching assistant was to assist a professor to grade papers and run errands. Because of my specialty in electronics, the chairman assigned me to teach three courses in electronics and electricity. My first day in class was for a senior class. The students in the class were just one semester behind me from graduation. Some of them were buddies in the basketball court or bridge games and we were good friends. Some of them had gone to movies with me just a few days ago. This assignment was a surprise to all of them because it was just so unusual.

When I walked into the classroom, they were astounded. They had to stand up and bow to me as they customarily did to all professors. I was highly uncomfortable under such circumstances. I felt all the eyes were staring at my mouth. My mouth became very dry and did not know how to get started. They continued to stare at me and watch every little movement I made. I felt like standing on a table naked with a thousand pairs of eyes watching. I wanted to give introductions to the course and set up some basic rules for the class. But I felt I was very clumsy at best.

"Good morning," I said.

"Good morning, Professor!" They responded by adding *Professor* at the end. I knew they were teasing me. My face turned red and forehead was sweating.

"This is the electronics 3 class. Am I in the right room?" I did not know what else to say.

"Yes, Professor." One of my old buddies was teasing me.

"We are not going to use a textbook in this class. Please be prepared to take notes," I said.

"But we have bought a text that was mandatory," someone protested. Gosh! I was wrong. The other class I supposed to teach did not have a text, but this class had one.

"Sorry! I goofed. Let's start over again," I said. Everybody laughed, and the ice was broken. That was how I started my thirty-five-year teaching career.

In the first few days or weeks in classes, I was very sensitive and nervous. When I saw someone smile, I thought that I must have made some stupid mistakes. That first class was so long; it felt like ten hours instead of just fifty minutes. Finally, the bell rang. What a relief! They stood up and bowed again until I walked out of the classroom.

I did much better in the next class, which was a junior class. I knew all of them, but we were not been so close as I was with the first class. I became more accustomed to being treated like a professor and started to concentrate on teaching subjects instead of being too sensitive and self-conscious. I was quite familiar with the subjects I taught. I needed only to prepare an outline the night before and walk into classes without any textbook or paperwork. I wanted to emulate the physics instructor I had admired so much when I was in high school. I was well prepared in subject matters, being patient to students' questions, and I was respectful to all students, even the ones that asked dumb questions. I thought I was very successful in that regard. I won praises from senior professors and respect from my students.

The first year was the teaching-practice period that we were obligated to do by the government for paying back the four-year support in the university. Our formal graduation date was one year after we had finished the course work. The graduation ceremony came after the teaching practice. Most of graduates were spreading across the island, but they all showed up for the graduation. It was just great to see old friends and compare notes on our teaching and social experiences after leaving the university.

The university had male-to-female student ratio of about three males to two females. The ratio varied from department to department. For example, the departments of arts, chemistry, and music had more female students than males, and the department of home economics had no male students. Dating pairs seemed more popular between students from different departments. In my class, there was only one classmate who dated a girl from a junior class in the same department. Most of the boys were interested in dating but were either too shy, lacked courage to ask for a date, or could not find an ideal candidate.

I had seen many pretty girls on campus, but I never had the courage to say hello to any of them. My buddy Sidney Yen was very interested in a girl from the English department whose family name was the same as mine. When we saw her on the campus walking toward our way, Sidney would ask me, "Hey! Buddy, go ask her if we could invite her out for a movie."

"She is your dream girl, not mine. You go ahead. I will support you," I would say.

But when she got closer, Sidney would become so nervous his face became bright red and he turned his head sideways.

Somehow, I did admire a few girls in passing but never had one who impressed me to the degree that girl did to Sidney. Sidney and I were good friends since the sophomore year. We became symbiotic ever since we discovered that when we bought a hot dog from a street vendor, Sidney would eat only the bun and I liked the sausage in it. That was how we established a close bond. We went out to buy lunch often and each of us would get what we wanted. Normally we would buy four hot dogs. Sidney would get three buns and I would get three sausages. Sidney and I graduated from the university in December 1957 and he never talked to his dream girl even once. I did talk to many female schoolmates and worked with them on many projects together, but none of them interested me enough. Dating any of them had never entered my mind, ever. There was simply no chemistry between me and any of them, I guess.

After graduation I was selected by the university to be a teaching assistant to help one of the professors. As such I had extra time to spend during the evening hours. I was thinking of something else to do. One day, in July 1957 a friend of mine name Yun-Sen Pan was visiting me. He told me there were lots of opportunities in business that just waiting for people to explore.

"I tell you there are tons of business out there. This is best time for us to establish a business," Yun-Sen said.

"Just what kind business do you think we can fit into doing?" I asked.

"Well something you are specialized or uniquely qualified to do," he said.

"Electronics is my specialty, but it covers a wide range of things," I said.

"I heard a lot of outfit are looking for transformer makers," he said.

"To make a transformer is easy but to find customers is another matter. Since you said there are lots of outfit looking for transformers that is good news," I said.

"So, what do you think?" He asked.

"I think it worth a try. What is the first thing to do?"

"I think you should register for a company and we go from there." He said.

Yun-Sen searched and found a small space for us and that was going to be our company's headquarters. We each chipped in a small amount of money to buy a desk and couple of Chairs. The rental was cheap enough so, we could effort it.

"How about a name for the company?" I asked.

"I always like the name Tien-Kon," Yun-Sen said.

"OK. Tien-Kon it is. I will register the company use it as the name," I said.

I started to check on how to register for a company. It turned out to be very simple. So, I register the company "Tien-Kon Electric Company". The next thing is to find a product to make. Since a transformer was in high demand, we decided to make transformers as our start up business. We needed to find someone with the experience of making transformer.

"I know of a man name Chang is very good with making transformers. Why don't I contact him and see if he is interested to join us," said Yun-Sen.

"OK. You keep me posted. I hope he will join us," I said.

He contacted Chang the next day. Chang was very enthusiastic about join us. I asked for a meeting to talk this business over. It was set in the next two days.

"I am so happy that you are joining us for this venture," I said to Chang, a man in his 30s.

"I am so honored to join you. I know your reputation as a teacher. Because I know Kwan-Hwa who is my best friend," said Chang.

Kwan-Hwa was my student in the university. From then on, the three of us was in a team to work for the company. Chang made some transformer samples for Yun-Sen and me to market. We took the samples and knocked on some doors, but the potential customers all wanted references which we did not have. Until one day, Yun-Sen met a buyer from a large company who was willing to try us out.

"Please get a sample or design for us to do the job," I asked Yun-Sen.

"They have promised me that they will give me a sample transformer to copy."

"Good! We will work on it after you get the sample," I said.

A few days later, we gave the sample to Chang and he started to make the tool for cutting the sheet metal for the transformer followed by winding the coils. In less than 10 days our sample units were completed.

"The sample was made by three subcontractors. I am sure they will like it," said Chang.

"I am so glad you get this done on time. I am going to give the samples to the customer. I hope he will like them," said Yun-Sen.

When Yun-Sen presented our sample units to the customer. He tested each of the sample and was very happy. As a result, we were granted the first order of Transformers. The work was divided into the sheet metal work which cut the sheet metal into core material and the coil winding work. Final assembly work was done by a third group. All three types of work were subcontracted to others.

"I calculated the sub-contractor's share and our own efforts the gain was minimal. We are almost at a loss," Said Yun-Sen.

"If the order keeps coming, we will have to do the work with our own equipment and hire workers," I said.

"That will take money. Where do we get the money to do what you said?" said Yun-Sen.

"Let us try to borrow money to buy the equipment first," I said.

We tried to borrow money from the banks, but the company had no assets as collaterals. So, we had to solicit from people that were willing to risk their money to invest in the company. We tried in many ways to find an investor, but no one was interested in us.

We kept getting the work from the same customer. The revenue was looking good, but the bottom line was not so impressive. At that time, I was ordered to report to the military training camp and had to give up the business.

"I am going into the military training camp now and it will be a one year and a half commitment. That leaves you and Chang to handle the business," I told Yun-Sen the day I received the notice.

"You do whatever you need to do. Don't worry about the business," Yun-Sen said.

"I will be totally isolated from outside world. What about the marketing part of the business?" I asked.

"Well, we could get someone like you to join us some time down the road, or we will just wait for you," said Yun-Sen.

"To wait for me is not practical. Why don't I just quit from the company and let you two do it. Since I invest so little in the company, I will just transfer my shares to you equally free of charge," I said.

"That is very nice of you. Tomorrow Chang and I will treat you in a nice restaurant to say good-bye to you," Yun-Sen said.

A few years later, the company was bought by a large company. Both Yun-Sen and Chang were doing very well in the transaction. By then I was in the United States of America.

CHAPTER 12

THE MILITARY SERVICE

The Republic of China draft board required all male college graduates to serve in the military for a year and a half. The service began with six months of rigorous boot camp training followed by one year of active duty. My male classmates and I, sixteen in all, were assigned to the army's infantry school in Fong-Shan, a southern town near Kao-Shiung. That was the one and only training session in the entire history of the training camp. Because in the previous sessions, all graduates were graduating in May and the training normally began in August. There would be no other spring sessions in the future.

We were the oddballs in a program that had started our freshman classes in the spring. Other than us, there were no other trainees in the camp, we were told. I was wondering how they could train so few students in such a huge military camp. At the time we received the order to enter the service, the sixteen males in my class were scattered throughout different cities in Taiwan. Each of us had to take a train or bus from our hometown to Fong-Shan's bus station and walk the mile and a half to the camp.

When I arrived at the camp that afternoon, I found we had another 117 trainees. They were the first graduating class of the Taiwan Police Academy. Most of the police officers were much older than my classmates. I quickly spotted two individuals in that police group. One was Lieutenant Tze-Shan Liang, the head police officer of the precinct near the university. The other one was Policeman Kai-Gin Lu, who had caught me a few times riding a bicycle without a light. Immediately after I spotted him, I walked to Tze-Shan and introduced myself. "Lieutenant Liang, do you remember me? You caught me riding without bike lights."

"Of course, I recognize you. How could I forget a rascal like you?" he said, laughing loudly.

We went to Kai-Gin and introduced me as well. We laughed about what had happened to us a few years back. Because Tze-Shan's hair was thinning, I called him Tri-Hair, the nickname from a cartoon bald character. We became very good friends while in the camp and continued the friendship into the next forty or so years.

I had been looking forward to the military training, not that I liked the training part, but this was the only way I could put my hands on a real gun. Ever since my early years living around soldiers, I had been fascinated to this man-made "wonder." Other than occasionally cleaning a gun for the soldiers and a couple of times firing a rifle round, I never had a gun of my own, not even a BB gun. A BB gun in China or Taiwan was very expensive. I knew I could do well with target practice, but there was no opportunity in the past. After we reported to the camp, the next morning, we were issued a US Model 1903 bolt-action rifle. My rifle was the serial number 710556, made in China, a beautifully maintained old rifle. I took it apart that day during a break after dinner. I gave it a thorough cleaning that it had never had before. I was anxious for the first "live-ammo" lesson. But I realized I had to wait for a while before they would give us the shooting lessons.

The officials in the camp did not waste any time on us. That first evening, the captain briefed us with all rules and regulations in the camp. The second lieutenant told us about the rigorous schedules in the days to follow. The rigorous training program suited me just fine. I liked the weapons, the rigorous exercise, and the strict military discipline. That was not true for most of the other fellows from my college class; they hated the weapons, the exercise, and the military discipline.

"What a waste of my life here! I just don't like the whole stupid place," Sidney Yen told me.

"I don't think this is too bad. After we started shooting the guns, you will like it," I said.

"No way. I don't like guns. You can shoot all of my ammo for me," he said.

"Really! I will take your offer. Don't forget your promise now. Okay?" I was thrilled.

The training was a no-nonsense real McCoy. At six o'clock sharp each morning, the bugle would wake us up. After fifteen minutes cleaning up, we would be lined up to take roll call. If it was not raining, the sergeant would lead us to jog up the hill then jog down on the other side of the hill and loop back to the barracks. It was a three-mile run each morning, timed for twenty minutes. It was difficult for many of my classmates, but we all got used to the jogging in a matter of a few days. Even some of the police officers were not well conditioned. Some of them had worked behind the desks too long and had equally difficult time to get started. During the first few days, many of them had dropped way behind in the morning jogging.

After jogging, we had fifteen minutes to clean up and change to full uniform for the day's field drills. I took the field training very seriously, but my classmates hated most of the training activities. We had to work under the sun marching, running, climbing obstacles, and jumping over ditches. The police officers were better prepared than the sixteen of us. But they also disliked the heavy drills in full uniform and carrying weapons.

In the third week, I finally got what I had waited for: live-fire practice. I was ready and eager, but my old classmates were not excited at all. They had never shot any guns in their life. Talking about shooting a gun, many were scared because they had heard that the recoil would cause a lot of pain on their shoulders. Some of them simply did not care about guns. All but me were so excited about the occasion. Several classmates including Sidney just handed me their ammunition when the drill instructor was not watching. I would shoot all the ammunition I had in my pocket and give the spent casings back to them to show the sergeant. My right shoulder did hurt at times, but I truly enjoyed every round of the ammo.

Each month, a target shooting competition was scheduled by the training command among all trainees in the camp. Sharp shooters were selected from the training group, including people from my class and the police academy class. The shooters competed as individuals. Because I was the only one qualified to compete from my college class, all my competitors were police officers. I found out that while most of the police officers were much better than my classmates, their shooting skills were quite uneven among themselves. Even with the few best police shooters, I could beat most of them in accuracy and reaction speed in all the competitions.

The competition always started on the first Friday morning of the month and continued throughout the day. It began with the fifty-yard fixed target. We had to use the rifle assigned to us. There were no special competition rifles in the camp, in any event. Five of the competitors received the perfect scores in the first and the easiest round of competition. The second competition was the three-hundred-yard fixed target. I was the only one who received the perfect score. The third contest was the moving target rapid reaction contest. The final contest was the popping-up and moving targets. I received perfect scores on one of the two quite difficult competitions. The

At the age of 23 in Military Training

police officers had the same feeling as I did—the moving targets were difficult to shoot at.

After the third month of competition, I was awarded a first-class sharpshooter certificate and received a ribbon on my chest. I thought my assigned weapon was the best rifle one could hope to get, although it was old and had been used in the past thirty years. I did align the sights and became used to the trigger pull. I could hit a very small target a hundred yards away with it. I turned down the offer from the captain for a new M1 semiautomatic rifle. I preferred hanging on to my old 1903 bolt-action rifle. It was like my old trusted pal. When I left the camp later, that rifle was the one thing most difficult for me to part with.

CHAPTER 13

MY NEW EXPERIENCE OF LIFE

My high school buddy Won-Shen Yuan, who was a second lieutenant in the Twenty-Sixth Ordnance, had to stay up north in Taipei for official business and could not get back to Kao-Shiung. He was supposed to tutor the two girls from Kao-Shiung Girl's High School who were preparing to take their physics class's monthly examination. He called me at the camp and asked me to substitute for him that weekend. The camp was about thirty miles from Kao-Shiung. I had to walk to Fong-Shan and take a bus to Kao-Shiung and walk more than a mile to find the address. It was a lot of trouble for me to travel. Besides, I was still very shy in talking to girls, but Won-Shen was my old buddy. I reluctantly agreed.

That Sunday noon, I took a bus to Kao-Shiung terminal. Won-Shen told me the house was only fifteen minutes from the bus station, so I just walked. When I found the address, I knocked on the door. A little girl of about ten answered. She told me that she knew who I was and led me into this Japanese-style wooden house. Her mother came out first and offered me a cup of tea. While I was sipping the tea, the student I was supposed to teach came out to the living room from

The Island Heaven

another room to meet this new tutor. After a brief introduction, I told them that I had to go back to the camp in two hours and would like to start the tutoring right away. The student, Ping-Ping Chiang, led me to a study next to the living room. We sat across a small desk facing each other. The other girl who was supposed to be here could not make it that day for reasons I never knew.

I started by asking questions on the subject, so I could get a right starting point. I was surprised how little depth the girl's high school was offering to its students. She was a very quiet person and I was quiet myself in front of a girl. I had not taken a good look at her since the introduction. When she was concentrating on reading the book as I requested her to do, I peeked at her with great admiration of her natural beauty. She had a very pretty face with unusually light skin and long and black shining hair. She was tall in the Chinese standard and was very evenly developed. In addition to all this, for unknown reasons, I found she was easy for me to talk to. I was surprised that I did not feel uncomfortable as I talked to her. After the session, her mother offered me a cup of soup with two soft-boiled eggs in it. When I got up to leave, Ping-Ping offered to walk me to the bus station, since she knew the short cuts. I happily accepted. On the way, we talked a little bit about ourselves. I found her a very pleasant person.

Guard Duty at the Military Training Camp

"I hope I can see you again in the future," I told her sincerely.

"If you travel this way, please come back to see us," she said with a smile.

I had a strange feeling that I would see her again soon. I had never had such feelings toward other girls before. Why was I so comfortable when I was talking to this pretty girl, as if I had known her for a long while? Might this be the fate?

After I went back to the camp, I called Wen-Shen in Taipei. He told me that he had intended to introduce me to the other girl. She was a very slim beauty. He had thought I might like that one. I told him that I liked the one I just met. Won-Shen was dating Ping-Ping's older sister, Chun-Chun, and had made some unhappy remarks about her mother. Then our conversation led us to some other things. We soon forgot about the whole event. Two weeks later, Won-Shen called again to ask me to substitute for him and said the family would like me to join them for dinner if I went. I gladly agreed to his request.

I anxiously waited for that Sunday to come. I took the bus and arrived in Kao-Shiung in early afternoon. I went to the house and met with Ping-Ping's two sisters, Chun-Chun and Ting-Ting, and her brother's family. Chun-Chun, at twenty-one, was studying in a college in Taipei. Ting-Ting, the youngest, was twelve. Ping-Ping's brother, Yu-Chang, thirty-one, was married to En-Fu Wu. They had three young children. Yu-Chang was on an out-of-town trip, and I did not meet him that day. The family was so big compared with my own. Her father was a gentle, quiet, and handsome man in his early fifties. He shook my hand and asked me to sit in the living room and excused himself. Her mother was very hospitable, apparently a strong-minded person, and was the main speaker of the house. She made the tea for me and excused herself to the kitchen. Soon there were just Ping-Ping and the two sisters accompanying me in the living room. I talked to Chun-Chun and Ting-Ting about their schools. We also made some small talk about movies and basketball games, but nothing remarkable. Strangely enough, I was not nervous at all when I was talking to the three pretty girls.

"How about let's look at the physics assignments now?" I asked Ping-Ping.

"Certainly. Let's go to the study." She led me to the study next door.

The tutor part took me two hours to finish. All the time, I was at ease. I felt I was talking to someone I had known for a long time.

"We have badminton at home. Do you play?" she asked me.

"I do, but not that well," I answered.

"Ting-Ting and Chun-Chun will you guys come play badminton with us?" she asked her sisters when she walked out of the study.

"Of course. We'll be there in a minute," Ting-Ting replied.

"Please get the paddles and the badmintons, Ting-Ting!" yelled Chun-Chun.

Ting-Ting ran to the closet to get the paddles. Ping-Ping led me to the front yard common to four of the houses in this residential compound. We played badminton until En-Fu called us in for supper. The days were much longer now than just a few weeks ago. At six o'clock, the sun was still way above the horizon.

We had this big dinner with many dishes of delicious food. But my attention was focused on her. That day, we sat around a large round table. Her chair was directly across the table from mine. She was facing the afternoon sun coming through a thin certain. She looked so beautiful as the subdued sunlight shined on her beautiful face, her lips were red without any makeup, her eyes were bright and sparkling, and her long, black hair flowed so smoothly and gently over her shoulders. I was just totally struck and attracted by her beauty and her gentle demeanor. I felt so fortunate to have met someone like her. Although I had not had much chance to get to know her better, I secretly told myself, on our second meeting in that godsend encounter, "One day I shall marry her."

I wrote a long letter to Ping-Ping from the barracks that night and told her that I wished to see her again but not to tutor her in physics. The reply came within a week and she invited me to visit her home again. So, I waited until the coming Sunday. Sunday was the only day the trainees could leave the camp.

That late morning, I set out to visit her at her home. I arrived just after lunch. Ping-Ping was home with her sisters. Their parents and En-Fu were out of the house. The four of us just sat in the living room chatting and drinking tea and soft drinks for a few minutes. We then played badminton with her sisters again in the front yard for a while. After the games, her parents came home. I went in the house and chatted with her mother and father.

"Is your father in the military?" her father, Pen-Yu, asked.

"Yes. My father is teaching at the National Defense University," I answered.

"How long is the military training in Fong-Shan? What do you do after that?" he asked.

"I have three more months to go in Fong-Shan, and then I will be assigned to an army unit for a full year of service," I said.

"You need to take care of yourself in the camp. It is not like in your own home," her mother advised me.

"Yes, I will be careful. Thank you for your kindness," I said.

Ping-Ping and her sisters joined in the conversations. Mostly that was small talk; with three girls, it was quite noisy but cheerful. I enjoyed this visit immensely. That was the new experience I had never had before—to be friendly with beautiful girls.

That day, I had an evening assignment as the sentry for the barracks at six, so I had to leave in the early afternoon. Again, Ping-Ping walked me to the bus station in Kao-Shiung.

"Are you going to college after graduation?" I asked.

"I plan to. But I don't know if I can pass the entrance exams," she told me.

"Well, have confidence. If you cannot pass the exams this year, you can take the exams again next year. You will make it," I said.

"What will you be doing after you are out of the military service?" she asked.

"I will go the United States of America for my graduate study," I said.

"How long will you be going?"

"I plan to get a master's degree in electrical engineering. It normally takes a year," I said.

"That is very exciting to go overseas and see the world. Someday, I would like to go too," she said.

"I would like to visit you again. Do you mind?" I asked.

"Of course, I don't mind. You are welcome to visit our home at any time," she said with a smile.

I felt very easy, relaxed, and comfortable in conversations with her. When we were saying good-bye, I really wanted to shake hands with her, but I was still too shy to touch her hand. Shaking hands with a girl was a big deal and a serious matter back in those days.

I wanted to see Ping-Ping more often, but the rules in the camp was very strict. I must have a pass to leave the camp. Otherwise, Sundays were the only days to leave the camp without a pass, if there was no duty such as the sentry duty assigned that day.

For me able to see Ping-Ping more often, I tried to figure out how to earn special pass privileges from the incentive programs offered by the camp. Before I met Ping-Ping, there was no reason for me to get a special pass for leaves outside the camp. Now there was every reason for me to get as many days passes as I could. *Well, I can shoot. Why not to get some awards from shooting competitions?*

I first earned a two-day pass by winning the monthly championship of the sharpshooters. The two-day pass meant that I had two days within a week that included Saturday and Sunday. The second time I got the two-day pass because I was the champion of the "fly catching contest."

The camp was infested by millions of flies. Each of the trainees was issued a flyswatter to kill flies. A contest was conducted to see who could catch or kill the largest number of flies. The winner would win a two-day pass. The rule required us only to turn in flies caught dead or alive. One would get credit toward a two-day pass based on the number of flies turned in.

"Lieutenant, do you mean we can turn in the fly's dead or alive in any form?" I asked.

"Well, as long as it can be identified as a fly, it will be counted," he said.

Before anybody else thought about the idea, I bought numerous sticky papers, put my name on the paper, and posted the paper all over the back of buildings. The sticky paper attracted the most flies. Within one day, there were so many of them stuck on my papers. It was not disputed that I had won the contest and thus the two-day pass. No rules were broken, but new rules were introduced. Sticky paper became a new category for competitors, and the number had to be one hundred to one against using the swatter. Most of the flies were eradicated in a matter of a few weeks.

When I was awarded a two-day pass, I would visit Ping-Ping two days in a row. Each time we became more comfortable with each other. However, in the old conservative society, I did not even give a thought of inviting her out to a movie or anything like that. Her parents certainly would not approve of it. I thought if I should ask her to go out with me, she had to get permission from her parents. I would be embarrassed by making such a request. I ended up spending a lot of time in their living room talking to her sisters or her parents. The only time we were alone was when she walked me to the bus station. Still, we maintained at an arm's length. It became a routine for me to visit Ping-Ping every weekend while I was in the boot camp for the remainder of the months. In addition, we wrote letters back and forth, but we never directly talked about affairs of the heart or any word as such. That was the way we were when I was in the boot camp for those six months.

What about my military training? The infantry school had scheduled a large amount of classroom instructions in addition to field training and weapon practices. Most of the classroom instructions dealt with political indoctrination. I was not interested in those topics whatsoever. Besides, I had some ideas about new weapons and weapon control systems that interested me much more than to listening to those dry and boring lectures.

Since I was exposed to small weapons in the camp, I started to formulate some concepts of war fighting devices that would have immediate application to current situations in Taiwan. At that time, the Communist frogmen often landed at night and sneaked into military camps in Kinmen, a frontline island only a few miles from the mainland. They would murder sleeping soldiers and use explosives to destroy ammunition dumps or heavy artillery pieces.

We needed something that could detect the invaders without seeing them and eliminate them from a distance. My ideas to counter such invasions were several, and they really excited me. Whenever I had the opportunity to write, I would try to put my ideas on paper. In the three months, we must have had over one hundred hours of classroom instructions. I spent at least fifty hours writing the four proposals of four different weapons and weapon control systems.

I presented my draft proposals to the director of research and development of the infantry school, Colonel I-Ru Muh, for his comment. He called me into his office the next day.

"I believe you have some good ideas in your proposals. You may have a chance of getting funding approval if we submit to the Ministry of Defense for you," he told me.

That was far beyond what I had hoped for. I had just hoped to have an opportunity to discuss the usefulness of my ideas. What the colonel said was to make the ideas into a research-and-development project and he would try to secure funding to do it. Wow! What had I done?

"This is just a draft to present my ideas. It is still full of errors," I said, a bit embarrassed.

"I will have a typist to put the proposals in the formal format. You just do the proofreading after the proposals are typed," he offered me.

"If you don't mind, I would like to review and make corrections before I give them to your typist," I requested. I knew that after typing, it would be very difficult to make any corrections.

"That will be fine. But remember you have only a month and three weeks left in the school. We need to submit all four proposals to the ministry while you are here," he said.

"I will get the review completed in two days," I promised.

"That is good. You just deal directly with the typist in my office. You are dismissed." I saluted him and returned to the barrack with the papers.

I felt time was very tight. I only asked two days to refine the draft. I was so very happy about what the colonel told me: getting funded for my research work. It was something almost unheard of in Taiwan those days.

With Ping-ping in Taipei

I requested the captain for a special leave from all activities for two days. He knew about the colonel's request and approved my leave. I worked more than sixteen hours in those two days to refine the four proposals. I was still unhappy with the writing, but I had to turn them in. I gave my refined draft to the typist Miss Liu. She was such a fast worker. Within two weeks, she had finished typing all four proposals. I spent four more days to proofread and make corrections to the typing and another week on the drawings. After the final typing and drawings were completed, I put my seal on the signature line as the principal investigator. The colonel's office prepared the necessary cover sheets and other parts of the proposal; he sent the package to the Department of Defense just a few days before we completed the boot camp training.

All the trainees were commissioned to second lieutenant of infantry in the army. The sixteen university graduates were assigned to serve in the army for twelve months while the police academy graduates were returned to their original posts. I said good-bye to my classmates from the university and the police friends.

"Tien-Ren don't let me catch you riding a bike without lights again," Tse-Shan jokingly said.

"Look, Tse-Shan. With friends like you, who needs enemies?" We all laughed.

"Come and see me when you are in Taipei. I will not give you a ticket," he said.

"In that case, I will see you sometime when I come back from wherever they send me to," I told him. We shook hands and went our separate ways.

We all reported to our unit directly. There was no time allowed for break to go home for a short visit because we were still in the state of war with the mainland. I wrote to notify my parents that I was not coming home after the boot camp. I figure they must be disappointed since they had not seen me for the entire six months after I entered the infantry school. The reason? Train ride from Kao-Shiung to Taipei took about twenty hours each way. Besides, I did not have enough money to buy the train ticket with the stipend I earned in the boot camp as a private of the army. My new assignment was to Small Scallop Bay south of Kao-Shiung.

I did make a short visit to see Ping-Ping at her home when I was on my way to Small Scallop Bay post. Because the order stated that my destination was classified information, I was not allowed to disclose it to anyone. She was alone at home that day. I was allowed into the living room.

"Ping-Ping, I came today to say good-bye. I can't stay long. I must report to my army unit down south immediately. If I can, I will write to you about my new job," I said.

"Where is the army unit?" she asked.

"I can't say, because it is a military secret. I will write to you as soon as I can," I said.

I was quite uneasy about keeping a secret from her.

"I understand. Please take care of yourself. I am looking forward to hear from you," she said with a hint of sadness in her eyes.

"You don't have to walk me to the station today. See you soon!" I said, extending my hand. She held my hand for the first time. Her tiny hands were so warm and soft. I felt like a surge of electricity run through my whole body.

"Good-bye!" she said softly.

Good-bye dear—I said only in my mind. I quickly walked away from the house and went to the bus station to a waiting Jeep.

I was assigned to the Reserve Corps stationed at the Small Scallop Bay as a second lieutenant in charge of half of the recruits to be sent to Kinmen—the Golden Gate Island. The camp had a nickname, soldiers called it, the Kinmen Hotel, hinting that soldiers who came to stay here were always shipped to the Kinmen front posts—to be bombarded by the Communist cannon fires.

The camp was about fifty miles south of Kao-Shiung and was not accessible by civilians. The Jeep took me through the small winding country road nestled in dense forest. Several watchtowers were seen hidden behind trees along the road. We were stopped at checkpoints at least three times before arriving at the barracks. There were several very large tin roof barracks sitting in the middle of nowhere surrounded by thick forests and wild growth of tall vegetation. A group of smaller buildings were the offices and sleeping quarters of the battalion and company headquarters. I was dropped off right in front of the battalion headquarters building. I took my paper out from my baggage and walked into the battalion administration office to report my arrival. The sergeant in charge, Li-Chian Tu, a forty some man and veteran of World War II, was on duty.

"Good afternoon, Sergeant. I am Lieutenant Cheng from the infantry school," I said.

"Welcome! Lieutenant, I have been expecting you. Please sit down. Have some tea while I process your paper," he said. "I will get you settled in no time."

"Thank you, Sergeant. Where is the battalion commander?" I asked.

"He rarely comes here. He is working at the regimental headquarters. We have Captain Yu in charge here," he said.

"How many companies and how many captains are here?" I was wondering. A normal battalion would have at least three companies and three or more captains.

"Oh! No. We have only one captain and you are the second-ranking officer here," he said. "Let me get the paperwork done. I will tell you over a cup of tea. How is that?"

"Sure, Sergeant." I was totally confused. For a battalion, there was only one captain and a second lieutenant? It was very fishy!

After Sergeant Lu finished the paperwork, he gave the list to a soldier for him to go to the store to get the items issued to me.

"Private Wang will send all of the issued items to your room. Come and have another cup of tea. I will brief you about the camp." Sergeant Lu pulled a chair next to me.

"This is not a regular fighting unit. Our duty is to safely take the new recruits to the fort in Kinmen or Machu islands," he said. "The captain and a lieutenant normally each take about five hundred soldiers on a troop carrier to the front as replacements and bring back soldiers who have been there for six months."

"Why take soldiers in just two ships?" I was asking a dumb question.

"Oh! That? Our camp has only the space to support 1,000 soldiers," he said.

"Is there any other camp like ours in Taiwan?" I asked.

"As far as I know, this is the only camp like this in Taiwan. That is why people call this camp the Kinmen Hotel. Come. Let me show you your quarters." Sergeant Lu got up and led the way. I had a private suite with a bedroom, a bathroom, and a small living room. What a fancy place for a greenhorn second lieutenant to live! Well, it turned out the suite was originally designed for a company commander but there was only one captain in the camp. Four suites like this were built when they built the camp as a regular battalion fighting force. Everything I needed was in the room, including an M1 carbine when we walked in the room.

"You should have everything here you need to get started. The carbine is issued to you, but there is no ammunition issued unless there is an emergency," Sergeant Lu told me.

"What emergency?" I was confused.

"Oh! That does not happen too often. When there are escapees on the loose, we will be fully armed to protect ourselves. When you are on a mission to the islands, ammunition will also be issued," he said. "The mess hall is down that way." He pointed to the building about thirty yards from my room.

"Thank you so much, Sergeant Lu," I said. "I will be needing much more of your advice about what we are doing here in the future."

"No problem at all, Lieutenant." He saluted me and went back to his desk.

With Ping-Ping in Taipei

When I first reported to work, there were no recruits in the camp. The .30-caliber M1 carbine assigned to me was a brand-new weapon. I disassembled and reassembled it several times just for fun. The food in the camp was just great because the veteran soldiers raised pigs, fish, and chicken for food. The extra meat was traded for

The Island Heaven

other amenities in life. I became friend of the captain, Shou-Chin Su, and several sergeants as well. They treated me nicely, because I was a novelty to them, the first college graduate and half-cooked soldier ever assigned to the unit. At the new camp, I could not find any private or public transportation to Kao-Shiung to visit Ping-Ping on the weekend. I sent letters to her, but I could not give her my returning address. When recruits moved into the camp, all outgoing letters were restricted.

About ten days after I reported to work, 1,000 or so recruits arrived at the camp. I was immediately issued twenty rounds of .30-caliber ammunition and instructed to load the ammunition into my weapon, since these recruits were to be sent to the frontline where the Communists kept bombarding Kinmen Island. The Communists also frequently sent frogmen, landing at darkness to kill our soldiers sleeping on the island during the night. All the recruits in the camp were very scared by such horrific stories. Some recruits tried to escape but all were quickly captured. There was no harsh punishment to the recaptured recruits after their escape failed. The only punishment they face was being put into a small classroom and lectured by a sergeant for couple of hours.

I was told the recruits could become violent if we were not armed. My assignment was to take five hundred of them to Kinmen aboard a troop carrier, the old LST. During an evening indoctrination session, a sergeant and I were given to the recruits.

"Why do you send us to the front to become cannon powder? We don't even know how to fight with any weapons," some soldiers asked.

"There really is no battle going on in Kinmen. You will be trained while on the island. We need you to defend our territory, and you are going to do it with other soldiers already stationed on the island," the sergeant replied. "The bombardment by the Communists is now on the even days but not on the odd days. Only a handful of people, mostly farmers, got killed in the past years."

As for myself, I was excited about going to the frontlines and what an experience it would be in my lifetime! However, I understood the anxiety among the young recruits. Most of them were farm boys who could not pass entrance examinations to high schools. That was the main reason why they were here. Most of them were eighteen to twenty years of age when they were drafted. This was totally different from the way soldiers forced young men from streets to become "recruits" during World War II.

Captain Su was ordered to take the five hundred recruits to Kinmen as he had done many times in the past. Due to some mix-ups, I had to wait for a few more recruits to be brought in from other cities before we were to board the second LST. The captain led the first five hundred recruits and two sergeants boarded the first LST and left the Kao-Shiung harbor in the early morning. It was August 23, 1959, when the LST left the Kao-Shiung harbor, navigating through the channel and into the Taiwan Strait. It was a sunny, calm, and very beautiful day. I was looking forward to being on my way to Kinmen in a day or two, I thought. After I sent off the first LST, I waved good-bye to the captain and the sergeants from the peer. Then I rode a battalion Jeep back to the camp. Like Sergeant Lu said, "We have done this a hundred times." No big deals and no indications of anything might go wrong.

Everything in the camp was just normal and routine. In the afternoon at about three o'clock, my field phone rang. On the other end was a voice I had not heard before, a major from Taipei, "This is Major Liang. Listen, Lieutenant. The LST with Captain Su on board was hit by at least two torpedoes and there are casualties."

"How is Captain Su and what about the sergeants?" I asked.

"I don't know, but you need to notify your people about the attack," he said.

"Yes, Major, I will notify our people in the camp and wait for further report. Any details what happened?" I was worried.

"We don't have any details yet. But I know that the casualty includes an officer," Major Liang said. My heart was sinking because I knew Captain Su was the only officer on board the LST.

"Oh no! I have a very bad feeling that Captain Su might be killed. Excuse me. I will talk to you later. Good-bye, Major," I said.

I had to put myself together and talk to all the people in the camp. I hated to announce the bad news when we were ready to send the other five hundred soldiers to harm's way. I was the highest-ranking officer remaining in the camp. I had to do it. I called all the sergeants. "I have unconfirmed bad news I just received from Taipei," I said. "The troop carrier Captain Su was on with our soldiers was hit by a torpedo this late morning. No details are in, but the major said there were casualties that included an officer."

"I am sorry to say, unless the information was in error, Captain Su is dead," Sergeant Su said.

With Baba in Uniform

In the camp, many of the sergeants had been with Captain Su for several years. He was most liked and respected by people working in the camp. It was very hard for me to watch these very tough guys crying. Tears also rolled off my eyes.

That day was the first day of the famous 823 fierce artillery battle between the Communists and the Nationalist naval forces that continued for a week. We only heard of the battle from the radio news report in the early afternoon. We never gave a thought to the news and did not know how close to home it was before the phone call came. The next morning, bad news came from the command headquarters that the captain and our two sergeants were killed in action when two enemy torpedoes fired simultaneously from two speedboats hit the stern of the LST. Miraculously there was no casualty among the new recruits. The LST was heavily damaged but managed to sail to its destination. We figured that the captain and the two sergeants were herding the recruits to go below the deck while they were still on the deck. The steel deck plates rolled up, knocking the two sergeants into the ocean and the captain was crushed between the rolled-up deck and the ship structure.

A day later, I went to the captain's quarter to gather his belongings for his family. He was usually a less organized person and hated to clean up his room and his desktop. To my astonishment, his desk was neat, his bed straight, and everything was in perfect order as if he had anticipated someone to look at the place. Did he have the premonition about his death? We could only speculate. The second ship was ordered not to leave Kao-Shiung pending future orders, for reasons unknown to me.

I was used to living among soldiers when I grew up. War and death were not strangers to me. I had seen enough and heard enough about the life and death of soldiers. But this time, the feeling was different, because the ones killed in action were my colleagues and friends. Just a day earlier, I was shaking hands with them when I sent them off to the sea. Two days ago, we were talking and joking while we had tea in the captain's quarters, and now they were gone and never to come back! It certainly shook me up quite a lot. I could understand what Baba had gone through during the two wars—seeing his colleagues falling one after another in the battlefields. It had to be dreadful and emotional for Baba during and after the wars.

While I was waiting for orders to depart for Kinmen, I received the order quite unexpectedly—to report to the college of engineering of the ordnance school immediately. I was hoping the order would come soon, but I was surprised by the urgency of the order. Before this order came, there were some pieces of news from the infantry school that the Defense Ministry was considering a grant, but there were no specifics. I took care of my departing process the minute I received the order and left the camp by a Jeep to Kao-Shiung's railway station.

I left my luggage in the train station and went to see Ping-Ping. She was home with her parents.

"I just received the order to report to the ordnance school in Taipei. I think my proposals are accepted by the Defense Ministry," I told her.

"Congratulations! It is the order you have been waiting for," she said. "When are you leaving for Taipei?"

"Right away. They don't give me any break," I said.

We had known each other for more than six months but had held hands just once. Without any emotional good-bye and just a longer than usual handshake, I promised her that I would see her again and hopefully very soon.

I took an express train to Taipei, arriving at Taipei's train station the same night. Mama was surprised but very happy that I was home so soon. She thought I would not be home for at least another week. Someone had told Baba about the transfer order from the Defense Ministry. Mama looked at me from head to shoes with big smiles.

"You look so handsome in full uniform," Mama praised me.

"Thank you, Mama, but I thought I was handsome also in plain clothes," I joked.

Baba came home late that night and was also surprised to see me. He was much relieved that I did not go to Kinmen. Mama and Baba both had worried about my assignment to taking recruits to Kinmen. They had heard about the sergeants' and the captain's death. I moved back with Mama and Baba in my old room before I went to the infantry school.

CHAPTER 14

THE BIG MEDAL

The next morning, I reported to work at the ordnance school. The campus was in the eastern part of Taipei. It took me forty minutes riding my bike to get there. I went to the administrative office and showed my paper to the sergeant on the desk.

"Where should I go from here?" I asked.

"You need to see Colonel Wang. He is the director of R&D of the college of engineering," he told me.

"Where is Colonel Wang's office?"

"He is in building 203. You cross the street to reach that building. You can't miss it," he said.

"Thank you, Sergeant." I left the sergeant and went to Building 203.

Colonel Wang was expecting my arrival. The secretary led me straight to his office. Colonel Wang showed me to sit in front of his desk.

"I am glad we caught you before the ship left the port. The ministry wanted the research and development plan as soon as possible. The funding had been allocated for three of the four projects you proposed. They are anxious to see the results," the colonel said. He looked like a very nice and honest man in his forties.

"The Defense Ministry is to provide the funding for the projects?" I was wondering.

"The Military Advisory Group of the United States will pay for the research through the Defense Ministry," the colonel said. "You need to write a plan on how you want to conduct the research work. Can you get it done in a week?"

Certificate of the Medal

"I will get the plan completed in a week! Where will be the laboratory for me to do the work?"

"Right here in the electronics laboratory across the street," he told me, pointing across the street where I just came from. "Major Po-Ling Du, the director of the lab, is expecting you."

"Yes, Colonel, I am going to see Major Du right way." I said. I got up from the chair, saluted the colonel, and left building 203.

Major Du was a burly six-foot, two-hundred-pound young man. He greeted me with a broad smile. "Lieutenant Cheng, how are you? I am glad to have you working here in the lab. We will help you with anything you need for the projects."

"Thank you, Major Du. I need to know how many electrical engineers and technicians you have here to help me," I asked.

"No engineers here, but I can get you two very good electronic technicians to assist you. You may need to get some assistance from universities in Taipei," he said. "The room next to Electronics Lab 1 is your office. That will be your home here during the time you work on the projects." He pointed to the small room right next door.

"I am going to draft a plan for the project. Would you review it for me before I submit it to Colonel Wang?" I asked. I was a bit disappointed by the lack of engineers and the sparsely equipped laboratories in the college of engineering.

"Major Du, I appreciate your willingness to help me. Thanks." I saluted him and left his office with a very heavy feeling in my mind. How was I going to do the work without the support of some brains?

It took me five sixteen-hour days to finish the draft plans to conduct the research and development work. I showed the plan to Major Du. He did not have any suggestions, so I submitted the plans right on the seventh day after I had reported to work. Now I had to wait for the approvals. While I waited for the ministry's approval, I had nothing else to do, so I just sat in my office for about a month.

The final approved plans were handed down to me. They had totally changed the management part of the plans. In my draft, I had requested four electrical engineers, six technicians, and technical consultants from the universities, but in the approved plans, there were three colonel-ranked directors, one for each project, a financial officer, typists, two technicians, etc. The only engineer was Second Lieutenant Cheng. I was very disappointed about the revision but there was no way I could do anything to change that. I guess the projects looked like a big fat pie to many people in the college. They wanted to somehow share a piece of the pie. Although I was disappointed, I was not discouraged by the washed-down plan. I had full confidence that I could get the development work done just by myself. I just had to work much harder. I told Baba about the projects and problems in the college.

"This is why we are not a strong nation. People are too selfish and greedy!" He sighed.

While in Taipei, I wrote to Ping-Ping almost daily. She wrote back just as frequently. Every piece of our mail was sent by the express mail. Each morning when I heard the motorcycle, I would rush to the door to greet the special delivery mailman. In the letters, we talked about our pasts, our families, and our thoughts toward the world. We were not romantic at all in our exchange of letters. I did suggest that we should see each other again whenever there was an opportunity.

I worked full time on the research projects with several on-call engineering staff members from the college and the technicians. The three colonels only met with me once a month to hear my progress report. It was more of a formality to justify their extra pay. Electronic parts in Taiwan, in the fifties, were difficult to find. Many of the electronic parts were under control by the military districts. I had to cannibalize parts from military surplus electronic equipment.

We built radio transmitter/receiver devices by using parts from WWII military radios that I went to an air force base in southern Taiwan to dig out from piles of junk. Transistors were not sold on the market and were obtained from dismantling several new portable radios. The infrared detectors had to be ordered from the US sources that took a long lead time to get. I worked on the project a minimum twelve hours a day, seven days a week. The two technicians were always with me whenever I worked in the laboratory. The staff engineers and administrative staff would just show up during normal working hours. They really did not have much to contribute to the projects, in any event.

Within the tenth month, all three prototypes were completed and off-line tested. I requested a test with live ammunition and explosives. The live test was conducted with the supervision of Colonel Wang and several staff involved with the projects. It was flawless. Colonel Wang reported the preliminary tests to the commandant of the ordnance school, General Fong, who in turn requested a final demonstration to the Defense Ministry and the US Military Advisory Group. A date was set for the live demonstrations; over a hundred people, including several generals, were invited to observe the tests.

The three demonstrations were to take place sequentially with live ammunition and explosives. I personally set up all test equipment, controllers, machineguns, and the banks of explosives just before the observers arrived. When the generals and the US advisors came, Colonel Wang introduced me to them, and I gave a brief description of what was to be demonstrated.

All three live demonstrations went as expected—flawlessly. A few days later, Colonel Wang told me that the defense minister, General Da-Wei Yu, was very impressed with the R&D results and would like to give me an award.

"Lieutenant Cheng, you have a choice of receiving the award in monetary form or a medal from President Chiang Kai-sheik," he said.

"I would like to have the medal," I replied without any hesitation.

About a month later, I was formally awarded a medal that was one of the highest military medals ever awarded to a civilian by President Chiang Kai Sheik of the Republic of China. The medal was not pinned on my chest by the president himself but was presented by the commandant, General Fong, of the ordnance school. A signed certificate of the medal was also presented to me at the same time. A story about the award was published on the front page in the national newspaper about a month later.

Medal or not, I was hoping the research products could be deployed along the key coastal areas in Kinmen and Machu, where Communist frogmen had been harassing the defense establishment. That was my motivation to start with, but I never heard of any of the follow-up activities because those were strictly guarded secrets in Taiwan.

After leaving the mainland over ten years ago, people in Taiwan were still forbidden to communicate with mainland relatives or friends; no mainland publication was ever allowed to enter Taiwan. Therefore, we really knew nothing about what was going on now and what had happened on the mainland in the ten years. Although we still chanted the slogans about overtaking the Communist regime and returning to the mainland, deep in our hearts, we knew it was not going to happen.

The street behind the central railway station was known as the "rear station" and no one referred to the street name, Yen-An Street. It was well known for the concentration of electric and electronics stores and street vendors on both sides of the street. One sunny morning, a Wednesday, I was in full army uniform, looking for an electronic part to be used in the research project. My attention was focused on shop displays while walking at a regular pace.

Suddenly, a military police officer stood in front of me saluted. "Lieutenant, may I see your ID card?"

"Why do you want to see my ID? What is the problem, Sergeant?" I impatiently asked him.

"You have just failed to salute a senior officer when you were walking toward and passed him. That is what we are trying to crack down," the MP explained.

"I was looking at the store displays, and I did not see any senior officer walking toward me." I told him the truth. The sergeant pointed to the major about twenty paces behind me and said, "I was walking behind the major and you did not salute him. That is the fact. So, Lieutenant, please hand me your ID. I must report this to the authority," he insisted.

I knew that there was no use to argue about it, since I indeed missed the salute to the major. I pulled out my ID card and the sergeant copied the information on his notepad. He then handed the ID card back to me and just walked away from me. At this point, I yelled at the top of my voice, "Stand still, Sergeant! Turn around." I walked toward him.

"What are you supposed to do when you leave an officer?" I barked at the top of my voice.

The sergeant's face turned pale and said, "Salute you, sir," he said in a weakened voice.

"That's right. But you failed to do that while you are on duty to crack down such behavior. You are knowingly violating the rules!" I yelled.

I was so loud, many bystanders circled us, and several of them cheered me on.

"Give me your ID card. I must report this to the authority that you ignored the rules while on duty," I told the MP.

While the sergeant was in shock, the major walked toward us. I saluted him.

He said, "Lieutenant, I have seen everything that happened here. I agree that you were looking at the displays and did not see me walking toward you. The sergeant was wrong by not saluting you. I suggest let us just forget the whole thing."

I really did not care whether the sergeant was to be punished or not, so I agreed not to report this incident, but I demanded to have the note with my name in it handed to me. I just put the paper in my pocket and saluted the major good-bye. I had such a sense of triumph and satisfaction. It kept me feeling high for at least a few hours.

CHAPTER 15

IN LOVE AND MARRIAGE

Unexpectedly, Ping-Ping's parents sent her to Taipei to live with her sister Chun-Chun in the summer of 1959. Chun-Chun was attending a business college near my parents' house. Ping-Ping was taking courses at a school. The school was established just for the purposes of teaching students how to pass the very competitive entrance exams. I was extremely happy with her decision to study in Taipei.

At that time, I was deeply engaged in the research and development projects, but I tried to find time to take her out for movies once or twice a week. We had a really good time walking the streets and the parks. All we did was holding hands while walking. That went on for several months. One day, after a movie, I put my right arm around her waist—the first time I had ever done that to a girl. Her reaction was also obviously strong. It was like a jolt of electricity went through her body, she told me later. I wanted to say romantic words to her, but I just could not get anything out my mouth. I wanted to kiss her, but I did not have the courage to bring down my dignity and to admit to her that I had been dreaming about kissing her for a long time. Eventually, in the following month, we advanced to a brief embrace in the park, without anyone else around. One day, while I held her in my arms, the smell of her and her soft hair brushing my face and ears, I could not help myself and kissed her beautiful and tender lips. We engulfed in kissing and forgot the whole world around us. No word was exchanged but the feeling was a thousand times stronger than any word.

We were in love.

I invited Ping-Ping to meet my Mama and Baba. They both liked her. I was going to be the first, in the family's history, to break a tradition that marriage was made by the young couple instead of between the two sets of parents. The arranged marriage was something very wrong, Baba told me in the past. While we were dating, the only complaint I received from Mama was that I spent too much time with Ping-Ping. That was true, but at that time, my heart and my thoughts were totally focused on her and nothing else was more important to me. I did get my work done on my job and did it well. I just did not spend as much time with Mama and Baba after work as I used to. That was true as well. I supposed all mamas and babas in the world were feeling the same way as their young were about to leave the nest.

Our feeling toward each other grew stronger every day. I had to see her every evening after work, unless there was an urgent matter relating to the projects. I would feel terrible if I did not get to see her that day.

It was the winter of 1959, my projects were completed, and my obligation to serve in the army was over. I went back to the university to teach again. Other than going to a different location to work, my daily routine was as usual, but my personal life was to be greatly changed.

Things developed rather quickly; I talked with Ping-Ping daily on the phone. She told me her mother had agreed to the marriage. We decided to get engaged in Kao-Shiung in a month or so. At the engagement ceremony, her mother did not attend, but there were hundreds of people at the banquet.

The Island Heaven

Wedding Photo

After our engagement, we exchanged a visit between Taipei and Kao-Shiung. Her two sisters were very excited about our new relationship. When I visited Kao-Shiung, I would take Ting-Ting with us to the movies. However, Chun-Chun was attending school in Taipei. When Ping-Ping was visiting me in Taipei, Chun-Chun would be with us most of the time.

Since I would like to go to the United States for graduate studies, I thought it was better to get married before I left the country. Ping-Ping agreed. I suggested to her that we get married as soon as possible so I could prepare for the trip to the United States.

We planned to have the wedding ceremony in January 1960 in Taipei. Based on the Chinese tradition to have the groom's family take charge of the marriage events, we leased the big conference hall at the university. Baba asked General Hsu, the commandant of the Defense University, to be the master of the ceremony, together with over three hundred friends and relatives. The president of the Normal University loaned us his sedan, a vintage Buick, as the car for the newlyweds to ride to the ceremony and then to our home. In the white dress, Ping-Ping looked just like a beautiful angel from heaven. Everybody at the ceremony praised her and congratulated us. I felt as if I were on the top of the world. Ping-Ping had her family members and relatives attending the ceremony. Her father, sisters, brother, sister-in-law and nieces and nephews were all there and seemed very happy for us.

The day after the wedding, the national newspaper published an article on the front page about the three inventions and about the award of the medal by President Chiang Kai Shek. It was a big surprise to everyone who knew me because I had not discussed with any of my friends the award. Nevertheless, we were all very happy about the coincidence. We had planned to travel to the southern tip of the island for our honeymoon. But the planned honeymoon never took place. Something we never expected had happened.

The day after our wedding, we found ourselves deeply in debt. Our wedding ceremony was supposed to be a very large and happy event, but it turned into a disaster that took Ping-Ping and me many years to recover from. It was not because I did not prepare for the wedding expenses. I had worked at three different part-time jobs in addition to my full-time job for a solid year to save up enough money for the wedding. I handed my savings, equivalent to one hundred months of my teaching salary, to Baba. I told him that was all I had. Normally this amount was more than enough to cover everything for a lavish wedding. Baba in turn gave all my money to his trusted old friend Chun Lin to manage the wedding ceremony.

On the wedding day, more than 350 guests showed up anticipating just refreshments as the invitation stated. The gifts were very light accordingly. But our manager, Mr. Lin, prepared over thirty-five tables of lavish banquet instead of just the refreshment. Mr. Lin was also very generous with our money; he even paid taxi fares and pedicab fares for guests attending the wedding. Since he did not keep a book or notes on the expenses, I did not know where we stood financially. As a result, the day after the wedding, we found we were deeply in debt; even the banquet was not fully paid. There were bills owed to other vendors as well.

The first day that was supposed to be the start of our honeymoon, we were busy taking our valuables, including our wedding rings, to the pawnshop. With all that, we could only pay a portion of the debt. I had to borrow from my relatives and friends to pay for the balance of the expenses. As for Mr. Lin, he just walked away and left the mess to me without even a word of apology.

We were devastated by the action of this irresponsible or dishonest person, but we refused to become discouraged by this unfortunate event. Since we had come through so many rough times in the past, we believed we could overcome the current financial crisis as well. We determined to work hard to clear the debt that was the equivalent of three years' salary of a college professor. I continued to work on the three part-time jobs and the full-time teaching job. The income was helping to pay part of the debt, but there was a long way to go yet.

We rented an apartment near my parents' house—about five minutes away by foot. It was a multifamily rooming house, very small, and lacked privacy. Because we wanted to save money to pay the debt, the rent of the apartment was the lowest we could find. Since the small apartment did not have a private kitchen, we ate our meals at my parents' house. As a custom, I handed over my monthly pay plus the rest of my income to Mama to manage the money for us. Mama would give us the allowance for the month. If we needed money to buy something extra, we just asked Mama for the money. When the money was accumulated to a certain amount, Mama would pay back part of our loan to our relatives or friends. Ping-Ping and I went to movies once or twice a week. Other than the financial mess caused by Lin, I thought we were very happy and felt quite fortunate indeed.

A month after the wedding, we traveled together to visit her family in Kao-Shiung.

I thought my wife was acting unusual those days. I was wondering if she had some physical problems but did not want to worry me. "Are you all right?" I asked her.

"I am fine. I just have a little stomach discomfort. There is nothing to worry about," she told me.

A few days later, as I came home from work, she had a mysterious look on her face. "Guess what the doctor told me today," she said.

Judging from the way she acted, it could not be anything wrong. "What did he tell you?"

"We are going to have a baby." She was gleaming.

"You mean we are going to be Mama and Baba? This is wonderful! It is a miracle," I said. I held her in my arms. "We are going to have a baby."

"I hope it is a boy," she said.

"It doesn't matter, a boy or a girl, as long as it's healthy. As a matter of fact, we haven't had a girl in the family for four generations. A girl would be a celebrated gift too." I was very excited about the news.

"Let's tell Mama and Baba. They will be very happy to hear this."

"Sure, you go ahead and tell them," she said.

We went to see Mama and Baba in the evening that day.

"Mama and Baba, I have good news to tell you. She is expecting," I said.

"This is big good news." Mama went over and hugged Ping-Ping. Baba was also very happy.

"I am so happy for the Cheng family. I hope you will have many children for our family. We have been very thin in the family tree. Since my grandfather, there has been just one son in the family," Baba said with a broad smile.

Our first son was born on a bright sunny day around noon late that year. Just before he was born, a brief but heavy thunderstorm hit the city, so we named him Ting, meaning "the thunder." He was a healthy and beautiful big baby. With breast-feeding and the Similac formula, he gained weight rapidly. Our center of life was shifted totally to the child. We moved back to live with my parents in their house. Our son then had the constant attention of the four of us. He was a gentle and lovely little boy who never gave us any trouble when he was an infant. As he grew to a little toddler, he seldom cried or made any fuss at all. We took him to visit the other pair of grandparents in Kao-Shiung once every other month. It took about six hours of express train ride each way. His uncle and his cousins just adored him; they had to fight each other to hold the baby. When he was about five months old, he was so lovely and chubby that his cheeks seemed to have dropped from both sides of his face. The baby had brought so much joy to our family. Ping-Ping and I felt very fortunate to have a son who never gave us any trouble.

My desire to pursue advanced studies in the United States had been in my mind since my college years. I really wanted to study in the most advanced country in the world in terms of science and technology. I also thought that without an advanced degree, I would be stuck with teaching at the instructor's level in any college. I had talked to Ping-Ping before we were married. She agreed with me that to get ahead in a teaching job, I needed a master's degree at a minimum. Now that I was all set with a lovely family, I had to do something in order to pave the road for a better life for my wife and our son.

"I think it's not too early for me to start the paperwork to apply for official approval for me going to the United States. It will take at least a year for the government to process the paper," I told Ping-Ping one day.

"It is never too early to start to process the paperwork. You know how slow the government people are. A year would be quite optimistic," Ping-Ping agreed.

With Mama and Baba

"The master's degree normally takes one year to finish. Because my English is not so hot, it may take a year and a half. Do you mind such a long separation?" I asked.

"Of course, I do mind the separation, but for the sake of our long-term future, I think it is worth the sacrifice. Do you agree?" she said.

"I agree with you. We all will sacrifice a lot from the separation, but it would be a very short time compared with our whole life following that. But I realize you will have a lot of burden to take care of our son alone," I said.

"Don't worry. Both sets of the grandparents will lend me a hand when I need any help. You just go ahead, get your degree, and come back as soon as possible," she said.

Once the decision was made, I started writing letters to request catalogs from several famous colleges and universities. However, before I worked on the applications to US schools, I had to obtain approvals from the government. I needed to go through a bunch of red tape set by both the provincial government and the ROC central government because I was financially supported for the four years of college. I thought it was fair to do so, but I did not know how long the red tape would be!

I had received many catalogs from big and famous colleges, but I only sent letters to two US colleges for application forms. Both colleges were highly recommended by my friends who had attended the schools. One was the Southern Illinois University at Carbondale, Illinois. The other one was Stout State College at Menomonie, Wisconsin. I completed the applications for admission to both colleges. I received replies from both colleges in two weeks. The I-20 forms and financial supports came within a month.

I was most impressed by the promptness of reply and the neat administrative process from Stout State College. Dr. Ray Wigen was the dean of graduate studies who corresponded with me from the very beginning. Stout was the smaller of the two colleges that I applied to. It had fewer than 1,500 students enrolled at the time. But my friend Feng-Chuan Chu had attended Stout and recommended most highly the faculty and the quality of the curriculum. Therefore,

I decided to attend Stout. I wrote to Carbondale to withdraw my application for admission after I made my choice. Both colleges had offered me tuition grants, but I had to pay for my living expenses that came to $700 at Stout.

I consulted with several friends who had studied overseas and returned to Taiwan regarding their experiences and recommendations for my own planning. With the I-20, I could apply for the government approval to study overseas. I immediately sent in my application to study overseas through the university right after the I-20 from Stout was in my hands. Because I was an employee of the provincial university, I had to get approval by the provincial education department first and then the Ministry of Education. The provincial education department approved it in three months and forwarded my application to the ministry. It was painfully slow just to find out at what stage of approval my application was in the Ministry of Education. I first went to the staff member Mr. Chang, who handled my application. He told me he had forwarded it upstairs. I went to see the department head in the ministry and asked him what happen to my application. He told me there were so many applications being processed that there was no way to find the whereabouts of my application.

I waited for almost one year but heard nothing about my application. So, I made an appointment to see the vice minister of education, Mr. Tuan-Kai Deng. He was very helpful and traced the application down where it was. It turned out the Mr. Chang, who received my application, was sitting on it. I was very upset and went to see the young clerk who handled the application.

"You are sitting on my application for a solid year. How could you do something like this?" I barked at him.

"I am too busy. You just have to wait," he said. He turned his head slowly toward me.

I was very angry. I really wanted to hit him right on the nose, but I knew that would be very bad for me. But I was still mad as hell.

"You are so incompetent, and you are a disgrace to all of the children of Hwang-Di," I told him in a low and calm voice, and then I walked out of the Ministry of Education building. Years later I learned that that young fellow was expecting gratuity from applicants. Since I did not give him anything, he just held back my application. What a corrupted young degenerate! He had wasted one solid year of my life just for a few bucks.

By that time, my patience was worn out. I decided to apply through a different channel that was open to me. When I receive the medal, I was told if I needed help to study in the United States, the government would assist me. I did not want to bother people unnecessarily and I was not sure where to ask for help, so I just applied through the Ministry of Education. This time, I tried to go to the executive Yuan that was like the White House in the United States. The secretary general, Dr. Sheh-Ping Chen, had known me since I was a freshman in college. He was also familiar with my work at the ordnance school. He personally promised me to investigate it. A week later, I received a letter from the executive Yuan. It had granted me a special permit to study overseas.

I was much relieved and happy by this special permit. I went to Dr. Chen's office and thanked him for his personal help. I knew without his help I might have to wait for another year or two if I were lucky enough by going through the Ministry of Education. If I happened to bump into another corrupt guy, I might have to wait for a long time or never be granted a permit.

My next challenge was to get my paperwork through several levels of red tape. The first one was the local district administration office to fill up all sorts of forms and obtain the "country exit" application form. This form had to be approved and chopped with seals by the police precinct and then sent to the Taiwan Security Command for security checks and approval. The process could take months. Fortunately, Baba knew most of the key officials and called them for assistance. The process took less than a week to complete. The last part was to obtain a passport from the Ministry of Foreign Affairs. My friend Ji-Tong Han knew a lot of people there and helped to walk through with my application. I received my passport in just five days.

Now came the more difficult part. I had to go to the United States Consulate to get a visa to enter the United States. A few matters had to be taken care of. The most difficult one was the proof of financial ability. I had to show them a bank note with enough money for me to live in the United States for a year. I had the offer for tuition support only. I needed to present a bank note of $700 for my living expenses, according to the clerk at the consulate. That amount was equivalent to thirty-five months of my teaching salary of twenty dollars per month; a full professor received thirty dollars per month. My aunt Tsu-Yun Chang loaned me $200 for my expenses and my mother-in-law borrowed $500 from her friends to make the required amount of $700.

The next requirement was also tough for me: interview by a consulate official. Because I had not had the opportunity to learn and practice spoken English, I could hardly carry on a simple conversation in English. I had very little time to prepare for the language requirement at that moment. I was concerned that my command of English was not good enough to pass the scrutiny by the United States Consulate, since I never took any English lessons beyond my freshman year. I was not yet worrying about how I was going to take courses in the States. I just wanted to go one step at a time.

I started to read English text and try to pronounce words with the help of an old tape recorder. The process to go abroad was suddenly moving too quickly; I had only a few weeks to learn English before my departure. I forced myself to memorize words and sentences in between work and all the pre-departure chores. My wife helped me by quizzing my vocabulary and grammar on the buses, walking on the streets, and every other opportunity we could find. I was quite optimistic that I would be able to pass the interview by the US Consulate officials. I was also confident that I could handle my schoolwork and get around the campus without too much problems. I was forever optimistic but not necessarily having much confident.

After I received my passport and prepared the document needed by the consulate, I called and made an appointment to be interviewed.

"Are you ready to take the oral examination from the US Consulate?" Ping-Ping asked me.

"Not really, depending on what he is going to ask me," I said.

"I believe you will do well. Just don't be nervous."

"I will try my best," I told her.

On the day of the interview, I got up early in the morning and took a bus to the United States Consulate building. I was very nervous because I had put so much effort into preparation for this trip. I could not afford being rejected at this time. My appointment was at nine o'clock. I was there at eight fifteen. I submitted my paperwork and took a waiting tag to be called. I sat in the waiting area facing a large wall clock. The seconds hand was moving ever so slowly. It seemed to be a long time when nine o'clock came. Some ladies came out from rooms down the hallway, but my name was not called. I became even more nervous. By nine fifteen, my name was still not called. Was there anything wrong with my paper submitted? Was the officer who was supposed to interview me late or sick?

Finally, at nine forty-five, the receptionist called my name. I walked to the window where she sat. She pointed to a direction and told me, "You walk into this hallway and find the third door on your left, and just walk in." I thanked her and proceeded down the hallway as instructed. I found the third door on my left and knocked on it.

"Come in, please," said a voice in the room.

I opened the door and walked in the room. A young American officer was sitting in his chair. When I walked closer to the desk, he got up and extended his hand.

"Good morning. My name is Bill Howe. How are you?" he said as he shook my hand.

"Good morning. I am Tien-Ren Cheng," I said. And I thought, *Gee! This American is so friendly.* I hoped he would not ask me questions that I could not understand.

"Please sit down and make yourself comfortable," he said, pointing to a side chair.

I sat on the chair and waited for the first salvo of questions. He flipped through my papers slowly.

"How long do you think you will need to finish the master's degree?" he asked me.

"I believe I can finish it in one year," I replied.

"Do you plan to stay in the United States and find a job to work there after graduation?"

"No. I plan to come back to my family after I finished my degree." I was telling the truth, which was what my wife and I had planned. He picked up his ballpoint pen and scribbled on my application.

"I wish you luck in the States," he said, handing me the stack of paper. "You can come back here in three days to pick up your other document and the visa."

"Thank you very much," I said. I could not believe I did pass the oral test so smoothly and calmly while my heart was beating so fast, as it was jumping out of my chest. It was much easier than people had led me to believe. I felt so relieved that finally my dream had come true and I would be able to study in the United States. Now I could take care of the preparation work for me to go abroad.

My admission was for the fall semester that normally would start in late August. But this was already June and I had not begun to get ready. I had talked with my wife that she and the baby would stay with my parents because she was expecting our second baby in January and needed help from my parents. Mama and Baba gladly agreed to look after them. I felt much better to be away for the year.

To fly to the United States, the airline ticket was $576 one way, an astronomical figure. That was more than two years of my teaching salary at twenty dollars per month. I had to find a cheaper way to travel. Through some friends' recommendations, I talked to a cargo shipping company. They offered me a one-way trip to the United States on a cargo ship to the United States for only eighty dollars, meals included. I was much relieved.

I had borrowed the bank certificate to show the US consulate. I also needed to take the certificate to show the immigration officer when I arrived in the United States. In my case, the financial certificate of $700 would bear interest while I kept it with me. I had to send the money back to my mother-in-law and my aunt as soon as I arrived in the United States.

At that time, I was still in deep debt from my wedding expenses. I went to visit and talked to a good and trusted friend, Ji-Tung Han, about my dilemma. He was from a very wealthy family.

"Ji-Tung, I need your help. But if you have any problem with it, you must let me know," I said.

"Tell me, what is your problem. We are good friends. Anything I can do; I will do it for you." He put his hands on my shoulders and looked straight into my eyes.

"It has to do with the debts from my wedding. I still owe about $400 to vendors," I said.

"That is not a problem. I will loan the money to you. There will be no interest on the loan. You pay my back when you can. I just wish you success in your trip to the US," he told me.

"Ji-Tung, you may not know how much it means to me. Without the money, I would not be able to go anywhere. I really appreciate having you as my friend."

"This is what friends are for. Do not forget me when you become successful someday." He was just joking; how could I ever forget about him? Ji-Tung went into his back room and handed me an envelope with money in it. With the money, I could get all the vendors paid off. If he did not loan me the money, I would not be able to leave Taiwan. My life certainly would not be the same.

After I had paid off all the debt, including interest for the last year to vendors, and paid my ticket for the ship, I saved about one hundred dollars in my possession to take to the new country as my initial living expenses. I was confident I did not need more than that amount, which was my five-month salary at the university.

With the passport, I now needed to get the visa from the US Consulate. All the students traveling to the United States had to go to the local health department to get a physical, including an X-ray. I took the X-ray film and other papers to the US Consulate for a US visa. I had to face an American official who would ask me questions. If my answers were not to his or her liking, I might be denied the visa. I was nervous because I did not know what kind of questions, he was going to ask me. What would happen if I could not understand his question? I was worrying while waiting in line for about two hours.

When it was my turn, I was guided into a small but neat office. A young, gentle-looking official was in his chair. He got up, shook my hand, and asked me to sit across the desk from him.

"Are you bringing enough money to live there while you attend the school?" he asked gently, as if he wanted to help me in some way. But I knew it was not the case.

"Yes. I brought the required $700 bank note, which was calculated by the school," I said.

I showed him the letter from the school and the bank note. He looked over the letter and the bank note, stamped my passport, wrote a line or two on that, and handed it to me.

"Good luck to you," he said with a smile and extended his hand. We shook hands.

"Thank you," I said. I felt so lucky that both US officials interviewing me were such nice, gentle people. That was not the case for many of the people I knew who went for the same interview. There had been many rejections in the past. Words on the street indicated that to pass the US Consulate was very difficult. Students who wanted to go to the United States really feared the interview.

At that point, I was ready to leave Taiwan. The ship was scheduled to depart in two weeks from the Kao-Shiung pier. It was the largest shipping port in Taiwan. One week before the ship was scheduled to depart, my wife and I decided to travel south to stay with her parents. The day we were leaving Taipei, Mama, Baba, and a group of friends, including my former chairman and professor, Mr. Koo and Mrs. Koo, came to the Taipei railway station to send us off. As I was boarding the train, Mrs. Koo stuffed a twenty-dollar US bill in my pocket. I wanted to return it to her, but she insisted.

"Please take this with you just in case," she said. At that time, she did not know how important that twenty-dollar bill meant to me later in the United States.

It was very difficult to say good-bye to Mama and Baba. Mama was not crying, but her eyes were red. I knew she had been crying earlier. She hugged me and held me tightly.

"Son, you must take care of yourself when you are alone thousands of miles away. You need to watch the weather and dress warmly, eat enough food, and get plenty of rest. We will miss you. Be sure to write home often." Mama broke up. I could not help but cry too.

Baba held up quite well, but I knew he was controlling his emotions. He put his hand on my shoulders.

"Son, you take good care of yourself. Don't worry about home. I will see to it that Ping-Ping and Ting are well taking care of. Write home often," he told me.

"Yes, Baba, I will do as you and Mama said. You both take care of yourself. Please!" I said.

"Good-bye!" Ping-Ping said. She waved to my parents and others seeing us off.

The train came into the station. Ping-Ping held baby Ting, and I carried the luggage up the train. Through the windows, we waved at our loved ones and friends as the train pulled out of the station. I was still engulfed in sadness.

"Mama and Baba are getting old and looked frail. While I am out of the country, I will be worrying about them," I told my wife.

"Don't worry about their health. They are only in their mid-forties. You just concentrate on your study. All of us will be fine at home. One year goes by very quickly. Ting will be two and a half years old when you come home," she said.

"This is going to be the longest year for me. Leaving you and Ting and my parents here, meeting all new people, not mention I don't speak their language well enough," I said. "It is going to be a long, lonely year for me. But I will be so busy studying and making some money to pay for my expenses, so that time will slip by before we know it."

"Don't forget to write and send us some pictures of you and the surroundings."

"I will write to you whenever I can, and I will send pictures I take in the United States," I promised.

The train arrived at Kao-Shiung on time. The whole family of my in-laws, except her Mama and Baba, were at the train station to greet us. As soon as we got off the train, baby Ting was held by his aunt. Chun-Chun grabbed my luggage. Ping-Ping and I were

The Island Heaven

there empty-handed. We took several pedicabs for the bunch of us to go from the train station to my in-law's house. At the house, we had a really good time together, talking and laughing with her sisters and her brother's family; the whole time I was waiting for the ship. My brother-in-law was much older than Ping-Ping. He was about ten years older than me. He worked for a chemical company as an engineer and was always busy with his business. He never participated in whatever the younger crowd was doing.

A week went by without any news from the shipping company. The ship was late to leave for routine maintenance. On the day it was supposed to leave, I was informed that it would be delayed for another week. I missed Mama and Baba very much, and besides, Chun-Chun would like to have my wire recorder for her schoolwork. It was a very logical excuse to take a quick trip up north alone.

"I will go back to Taipei to bring the recorder back. It will take only a day or so," I told Ping-Ping.

"It's a good idea. I need you to bring my sweater down here. It gets cold at night here," she said. "You may want to visit with Mama and Baba a little longer there. I know you missed them."

"You are quite right. I will leave today. Might be back here the day after tomorrow," I said.

I took the morning train to Taipei and arrived in the late afternoon. Mama and Baba were surprised to see me back. I explained about the delay of the cargo ship. At home, I spent the next day and evening talking to Mama while helping her on house chores. I also spent time chatting with Baba after he came home from work.

The next morning, when I was leaving, I begged them not to come out of the house. I knew emotionally it would be too much for Mama, Baba, and me. I wanted just to walk out of the house like I did thousands of times. I took the wire recorder, just said a quick good-bye, and rushed to the train station. Deep inside of me, sadness and the fear of not seeing them again had cut my guts into pieces.

Back in Kao-Shiung, I expected the ship to depart any day. I needed to be able to get on board at a moment's notice. I always liked to travel light. I only packed a few pairs of underwear, two dress shirts, a suit, and some toiletry items in a small canvas suitcase.

I knew the weather in Wisconsin was very cold, so I brought a heavy long coat with me. I also bought a few pirated electrical engineering textbooks from street vendors at one dollar per book. The books fit into a cardboard box that was just a bit smaller than the suitcase but was much heavier. The September weather in Taiwan was still hot during the day. It was hard to imagine in just a month or so, I would be in a place that was freezing cold.

I was curious but did not have any idea of what kind of ship was I going to board. Because the ticket was very inexpensive, I wondered if it was a ship with steel construction or an old wooden ship. Since it was a cargo ship, what kind of living condition was on the ship? How fast could it go, and how long would it take us to reach the United States of America?

CHAPTER 16

LEAVING TAIWAN

The note from the shipping company finally came by a hand-delivered notice. The ship departing date—September 12, 1961—was only two days away. The night before leaving, my wife and I stayed up late talking about what to do while I was away.

"We will miss you terribly. But we will be fine here, and don't worry about us. You need to take good care of yourself," she said repeatedly. She did not cry in front of me, but judging from the looks of her eyes, I knew she did a lot of sobbing.

"You will be living with my mom and dad, so they can help with the baby. Besides, you can keep them company, so they will not be too lonesome," I said.

Going to the United States for an advanced degree was my dream when I was in college as a student. But that was just a dream. In Taiwan during that period, going to the United States was the exclusivity of rich people or high government official's children. I had no money or the influence. So that was just a dream. Now that I was working in a university as a teaching assistant, my desire to go study in the United States became stronger than ever. I had to find a way to go.

After I got the visa, I had to arrange for my travel to the USA. My first choice was flying to the USA, but the airline ticket at the time was $576 one way from Taiwan. With my monthly salary of twenty dollars, that was an impossible amount I had to produce. And I had no place to borrow such a huge amount. Therefore, I started to look for alternative ways. I started to check with my friends who had done this before. Some friends suggested that I go through the water instead of flying. It was a good alternative since I was under no pressure to go there at certain time.

I started to look around for opportunities. One day, I happened to notice a newspaper's corner. There was an announcement that a cargo ship was taking passengers. That we had a name called the passengers "the yellow fish." Normally I would be suspicious about it. But now I was desperate. I didn't care what it meant to be a "yellow fish," if it would take me to the United States. I took a cab and went to the shipping company.

"Sir, do you have ticket to go to the United States of America?" I asked one of the clerks on duty.

"Yes. We have only one ticket left. Do you want to buy it?" the clerk asked me.

"How much is it?" I asked.

"It will cost you eighty US dollars. Both room and board are covered," he said.

"I want it. Can you hold the ticket for a couple of hours? I will go home to get the money to pay for it."

"I cannot wait for you, if you don't come back," the clerk insisted.

"Okay, I have forty yuan here. You hold the ticket for me for no more than two hours. Is it okay?" I begged. At the time, each dollar equaled forty yuan.

"Okay. Be back within two hours, or I will sell the ticket to the next customer," he said.

So, I went home and got the eighty dollars and then bought the last ticket. The shipping company clerk told me that the ship was undergoing routine maintenance and would take some time to finish. I would be notified when the ship was ready for sailing. That was fine with me. That was in July 1961. The school's second quarter would start in November. So, I had plenty of time to wait.

Taiwan was not my homeland. I came to the island country when I was fifteen years old from mainland China. In Taiwan I lived until I was twenty-seven years old.

My memory of my teenager years to adulthood was with the mainland and Taiwan combined. To me, my homeland was the mainland, for we still hoped that the Chiang Kai-Shek's government would someday return and rule there. We were here temporarily. But Taiwan was the land my loved ones lived in.

I had sadness and excitement—mixed emotions. In two days, my wife and I reviewed all things to do and talked about the future. Thinking about the long separation, my wife and I were very sad. But when we thought about the unknown future, we were scared and having lots of hope at the same time. We talked about how lonely we would be, but two years could go quickly. The baby was now one year and two months old. When I came back, he would be two and a half or three years old. I hoped he could recognize me. We then dozed off for a while, and soon the sun came out. It was time to leave for the shipping dock.

It was a bright, sunny day and very warm in the morning. We hired five pedicabs to transport myself, my wife, the baby, and the whole family of my in-laws to the pier. It took only thirty minutes. When we arrived at the pier, there was a ladder going up to the ship. My father-in-law and brother-in-law helped me bring the two pieces of luggage aboard the ship and wanted to see how the cargo ship was arranged to take passengers for the sixteen-day trip across the Pacific Ocean.

The ship was a WWII Liberty ship called EC2, which was used to carry war supplies and troops between the United States and Europe. It was a large ship of over 10,000 tons. The major portion of the ship was the cargo bay, which was in the front section and rear section of the ship. The superstructure was in the midsection of the ship. From the deck, there were three stories of the structure. The superstructure consisted of the bridge on the top, the living quarters of the officers, and the living quarters of the sailors on the second floor and first floor. Although it was very old, by the looks of it, it was almost new. It must have been well maintained. I was glad to note that the ship was steel constructed and not a wooden one that I was worried about. It had a new paint job, and the engine was overhauled recently. We all felt that we would be safe on board this sturdy ship for a journey to the United States.

"This is a good ship. I think you will be safe to take it," my brother-in-law said.

"I think so too. My trip is just sixteen to eighteen days across the Pacific. I will be there in no time," I said.

At twelve o'clock sharp, the captain ordered all visitors to leave the ship. I said good-bye to each of my relatives on the ship. Of course, the most difficult ones were with my wife and the baby. We hugged for the last time before I returned. I kissed the baby on the cheek and held him for a few seconds. We controlled our emotions as they slowly walked off the ship. I watched them leaving the ship. My wife turned her head several times before they got to the platform where they could watch the ship leaving.

The ship quickly got underway. It immediately made a ninety-degree turn toward the channel. I ran from the portside to the stern and waved at my dear ones. Suddenly the ship sounded off a loud whistle and my son cried louder than I'd ever heard him before. Tears streaked down my cheeks uncontrollably as the figures on the shore became smaller and smaller. I began to think how life would be in separation and how lonely we would be before we reunited. For me, daily life would be so busy in dealing with what was coming to me, but for her, the daily life would be so boring indeed. She would go to live with my mom and dad at home in Taipei, where the baby would be in good hands.

As the passengers gathered in the lower deck of the ship, we were briefed by the first mate of ship. He introduced himself as Mr. Liu, and then he let the passengers introduce us.

"I am Tao Lee, from Taipei, and I am going to New York," said Mr. Lee.

"I am Kwang-hwa Wang, from Tainan, and I am going to California," said Mr. Wang.

"I am Tien-Ren Cheng. I am from Taipei, and I am going to Wisconsin," I said.

"I am Mrs. Goldberg. I am from Los Angles. That's where I am going," Mrs. Goldberg said.

Then the first mate gave us the keys to our rooms. "Mr. Lee, you stay in cabin 5. Mr. Cheng, you stay in cabin 2 with Mr. Wang. And Mrs. Goldberg, stay in cabin 3. Here are your keys. Be sure to take good care of them. Don't lose them. If you should lose them, there will be a fine of five yuan," the first mate said.

I shared one of the cabins with Mr. Wang. The other male passenger, Mr. Lee, shared a room with a lieutenant of the ship. The lady passenger, Mrs. Betty Goldberg, was a grandmother returning to the United States after visiting her son's family in Taiwan. She took one of the officer's cabins by herself.

We then settled into our own cabin. It was a small room. Its size could be no more than sixty square feet. There were two beds in the room and a head table separated the two beds. Mr. Wang asked me which bed I wanted. I said I did not mind, so he took the one at the fore end of the cabin and I took the one at the aft end of the room.

Mr. Wang was a strange fellow. He seldom talked. If he talked, judging from his facial expressions, he seemed suffering pain somewhere. So, I just minded my own business and left him alone. On the other hand, Mr. Lee was a normal fellow. I would meet him on the deck or the dining hall and chat about our current events and future. Too bad we were assigned to different cabins.

Our cabins were on the second floor on the opposite side of the ship from Mr. Lee's and Mrs. Goldberg's. On the second floor, there were other four cabins to which we did not know what functions that served. I only know four officers stayed in the cabins on the second floor. The captain's cabin was on the third floor with the first mates. On the second floor, there was also the dining hall just three doors down from my cabin.

After the ship was on the high sea, Captain Ouyang gathered the passengers in the dining hall and introduced the five officers to the passengers. We also introduced ourselves and where we were going. Most of the officers were in their late twenties and early thirties. Captain Ouyang was the eldest man on board the ship. He was forty-six years old, same age as my father. Mrs. Goldberg looked like she was in her fifties. I was twenty-seven years old and the other two fellows were twenty-four years old.

"You are our passengers. We have the duty to protect you and treat you well as our customers. The ship's entire crew and I welcome you on board and hope this will have a smooth and relaxed journey. This is the dining hall. We will eat here all three meals. And it will serve as our meeting room. Hope you will enjoy this trip," the captain said.

This was a cargo ship. Therefore, amenities were very simple. There was a dining hall for both the officers and sailors. It had two dozen tables that seated four people and were all anchored to the floor. A lager table was used for food and utensils. A television set was installed in the dining hall, but there was not any station to watch. The first mate, Mr. Liu, told me that we could watch TV programs when the ship got closer to American shores. I had never seen a TV program before, since there were no TV stations in Taiwan at that time. Meals on the ship were first-class, from my point of view. We had three meals a day. Both lunch and dinner were served with chicken drumsticks and pork chops. Breakfast consisted of white-flour bread and some pickled vegetables and dried peanuts. Such good and rich food was not easy to come by while I was in Taiwan. Fruits were also available on the ship, free to all passengers.

The captain gave the four passengers a personal tour to the bridge and the communications room. I was very much interested in all those marine gadgets on the ship, especially those of communications and radar equipment. But there was no chance for me to ask many questions during the group tour. I had to contain my curiosity to a later time. The captain was such a nice person that I looked up to him like my father.

I made friends with the captain's dog, a German shepherd named Max. Max was a five-year-old big dog, very smart, and playful. He only stayed in the dining hall and would not go anywhere without his master, the captain. When I became bored with looking at the sea and the blue sky, I played with Max. The other two passengers, Mr. Wang and Mrs. Goldberg, were quiet types and loners. Mr. Lee was different. He was friendly and talkative. I asked him where he was going. He told me he was going to New York City to attend Columbia University.

"Are you going there for your master's degree?" I asked.

"Yes. But I intend to pursue my doctorate degree afterward," he told me.

"Are you married?" I asked.

"No. I will not get married until I received my doctor's degree. I am not in a hurry to get married, because I have two brothers who are married and have children," he said.

"Well, good for you that you are free like a bird. I am the only child at home, so I am obligated to my parents to have my children to continue the family name," I said. "I am going for my master's degree only and going back to teach."

"One must do what one has to do. I wish you luck in the United States. Maybe you will change your mind when you are in the United States," Mr. Lee said.

Mr. Wang and Mrs. Goldberg spent their time in their cabins, reading books and magazines. Throughout this trip, I never became acquainted with them, even though Mr. Wang shared the cabin with me. I befriended Captain Ouyang, the first mate Mr. Liu, Mr. Lee, and several sailors. I was invited by the captain to the bridge to watch how to drive a ship. I gladly obliged such invitation and spent some time on the bridge after the ship was underway.

Normally there were four or five people on the bridge. It would be the captain or the first mate leading the group and one officer or trainee would be handling the helm. That seemed to be an easy job. I observed. Looking from the bridge through the windshield, the ship was cutting through the ocean smoothly.

CHAPTER 17

Typhoon and the Seasick Shepherd

It was a sunny and calm day when the ship steamed northeast in the Pacific Ocean. The sky was deep blue, and the seawater was calm and clear. I watched the ocean and saw the occasional flying fish and dolphins going by the ship. September in the South Pacific was still very warm. With the ship steaming at ten to twelve knots per hour, when I stood on the deck, it was cool and comfortable.

My mind was filled with hopes and I imagined what it was going to be like in the United States. With my language barrier, how could I communicate with people? I did not go through the preparations like others who came out of Taiwan. I was in a hurry to go through the necessary steps while teaching to make a living. I did not have my English prepared as I should. All I could do now was to deal with it when it happened.

Financially, I carried $120 of my own money. I thought that would last me for a while. In Taiwan I could spend less than one

The Island Heaven

dollar for a comfortable day. I mean food. I figured when I arrived in the city of Menomonie, Wisconsin, I should be able to find a job to repair radios or something before I exhausted my cash reserve. Besides, I had a tuition and room scholarship; all I needed to take care of was my food bill. I was confident enough that I was not overly worried.

The good weather only lasted for six days. In the afternoon of the seventh day, I saw all hands-on board were busy doing something on the deck. A sailor told me that the water would become very rough soon. But the weather still seemed to be very nice to a layman like me at that moment. I was most curious about what was going on and what was going to happen, so I stayed on the deck and watched the sailors tie down things and move items around to a more secure position.

Wind speed from the starboard direction was gradually picking up. Waves also started going higher by the minute. I saw the southeast corner of the sky becoming darker and the clouds growing thicker. The ship became unstable as the wind and waves became stronger. Deckhands secured all the moveable objects on the deck with ropes. Flags were raised to signal strong winds. I figured there had to be a storm forming and it would be hitting us soon.

"All passengers, please go to the dining hall now," the captain announced in the intercom.

This was new to us. So, we walked to the dining hall. There, a few officers were gathered waiting for us.

"It is imminent that Typhoon Bass will cross paths with the ship. You all need to be careful and follow the rules on the high seas, but you need not be alarmed about the ship's safety. I will see to it that we get out of the storm safely," the captain said calmly.

"Oh my god! The typhoon is to hit us! How come we did not have a warning before we left the port?" Mr. Lee asked.

"Well, I guess when we left Kao-Shiung, the typhoon was just forming. No one knows what it is going to become. So, we just took a chance that the typhoon would bypass us," the captain said.

"Is this typhoon big or just a small storm?" I asked.

"I don't know. The message we received only stated a typhoon was to cross our path but did not say how strong it is," said the captain.

"Is the typhoon a big one or just a small typhoon?" again asked Mr. Lee.

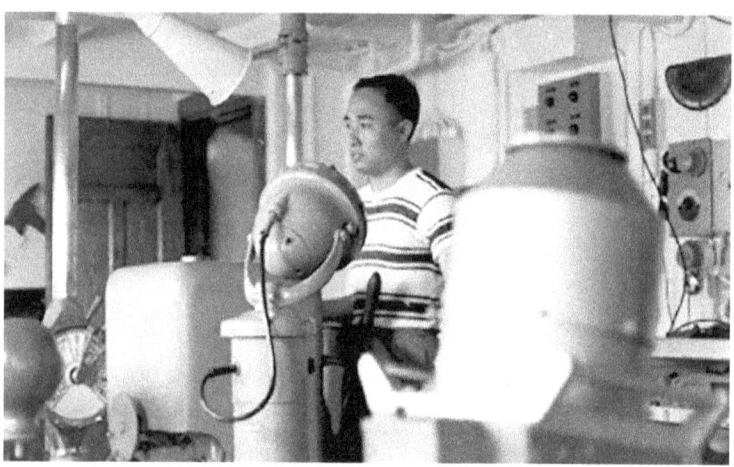

On Board the Ship and Behind the Helm

"We don't know that until we are in there. The warning system is not that good at this time," the captain said.

"Can we run away from it?" I asked.

"I am afraid not. It is too late for us to do that now," the captain said.

"Where should we be staying during the typhoon?" Wang asked.

"You can stay in your cabin and shut the door tight. Be sure nothing will be tipped over as the ship rolls," said the captain.

All the other passengers went back to the cabin as instructed.

"May I stay on the bridge and watch?" I asked the captain.

"Sure, you may. Just be careful," he said.

After the briefing, the captain and I went up to the bridge. There were two staff people on duty. They struggled with this helm as the wind was pushing the ship in different directions. Soon the sky became very dark. The strong wind was howling loudly. Thick clouds covered the entire ocean. With the heavy rain whipping sideways on the ship, the loud noise was overwhelming. From the bridge, I could not see anything in the ocean except the water and the heavy rain. All deckhands went down to their quarters after the preparation work was done. The captain was concentrating at the huge compass installed just in front of the helm, turning the helm left and right to keep on the bearing.

"The sea will become heavy soon. The waves will become higher, so the ship will take some beating," the captain told me.

"When will the typhoon really come?" I asked.

"Perhaps in the morning hours, a few hours from now. For now, it is just the rain and some winds," the captain said.

As there was nothing for me to see or to do, I said good night to the captain and went back to my cabin. Wang was in bed since a while back. I didn't know whether he was sleeping or not, but I dared not to disturb him. This night was horrific. I felt the roll of the ship and the screaming of the wind. I feared when the typhoon became strong what it would be like. I had a bad night while I hardly fell asleep. I was afraid when the typhoon really came what was going to happen. All night I heard the wind-whipping sound and felt the roll of the ship. I could not fall asleep. But near three o'clock, I finally fell into a deep sleep.

The next morning, around six o'clock, I was awakened by the loud shirking noise of the wind and the sound of waves crashing against the ship. The ship was vibrating violently after each crash of seawater. The ship was rolling violently. Objects in the cabin were thrown across the floor in a random fashion and thrown backward. I tried to get up and was thrown back to the bed. I finally struggled to put on my heavier jacket, ready to go to the bridge to see what the storm looked like. Wang was curling in bed and looked sick.

"Are you all right?" I asked him.

"I think I am sick. I feel nauseous," he said.

"Can I get you anything?" I asked.

"No. Just leave me alone," he said, covering his face with the blanket. I knew he had to be very sick and uncomfortable at the time.

I tried to walk toward the bridge. The bridge was one floor higher than the dining hall and one could reach the bridge through an inner path and an outer path. I chose the inner path, for the outer path was very dangerous at the time. The ship was rolling forward and backward very violently. Each time when it was rolling backward, I had to climb, sometimes at a very steep angle. When it was rolling forward, I felt I was to drop on the floor. Even by taking the inner path, I had to hold on tightly to railings to keep myself from falling to the floor or bumping onto the ship structures.

It took me a few minutes just to reach the dining hall. I opened the dining hall's door and walked in. The only person there was the captain and his dog, Max. I walked into the dining hall and had to hold on to the table in order to stable myself. I sat down across the dinner table from the captain. We had some tea and some light breakfast. The utensils would not stay on the table, so we had to eat with our hands.

"Tien-Ren how are you this morning?" he asked me.

"I am fine, and how about you?" I asked.

"I am in good shape, but just about all of my officers and sailors became seasick in the storm and we have just started entering the edge of the typhoon. It will be rougher later for at least twenty to twenty-four hours before we leave the effect of the typhoon," the captain told me.

"Wow! It sounds like a big typhoon," I said.

"It is big. But we will make it. I am going to take over the control of the ship soon. I don't know how my guys are doing now," he said as he got up.

"May I go with you to the bridge to watch you guide the ship in the storm?" I asked him.

"Of course, you are welcome to keep me company, as long as you can keep yourself from getting seasick," he said.

"I have been on ships several times before and I never got seasick," I told him confidently.

"Let's go up there now," he said, and he led the way to the bridge. Max followed. Again, we had to struggle to walk the distance and climbed the stairs to the bridge.

On the bridge, the two officers looked very pale from seasickness. The captain relieved them and took over the control of the ship.

"Come up here in two hours. If I need you sooner, I will call you on the intercom," the captain told the two officers.

"Yes, sir," they said, and they quickly left the bridge.

I stood right behind one of the windshields next to the helm and held on to a rail just underneath it. The ship was heading at an angle toward the waves in the angry ocean. Even with its 10,000 tons of weight and size, it was like a small leaf being tossed up, down, and sideways in the vast ocean. Then the waves would wash over the windshield, making a big impact and sound like a big explosion. I had held on the handrail tight; otherwise, I would be on the floor of the ship. I was fighting to gain balance when the ship was rolling.

As I looked through the windshield, I saw the bow went slowly lower, lower, lower and was listing to the left. I thought, *Gee, this is it! We are going to go below the water this time.* At that moment, a giant wave washed through the ship's top up above the windshield. And the sound of the water hitting the windshield was deafening.

"Captain! Look! Are we going down and never going up again?" I was frightened.

"It will come up. Don't worry!" The captain's calm voice made me feel better.

Indeed, at one point, the bow came back up higher and higher slowly then dropped down again. When the bow was up in the air, the storm wave hit the bottom of the ship, sounding like a giant explosion, and the shock wave could be felt throughout the ship. This up-and-down cycle repeated endlessly. The force of the wind and the waves was mercilessly tossing the ship around in every direction, and there seemed to be no end to it. The captain occasionally shouted orders to crew in the engine room.

"Are you afraid?" the captain asked me while handling the helm.

"Yes, Captain Ouyang. I am afraid the ship may go down and not to recover from that," I said.

"No. It doesn't happen that way. If the ship does not take in water, we are safe," he said.

"How do you know that we are taking in water?" I asked.

"The sailors are on full alert, although most them have seasickness. We will know if there is a leak," he said. I did not detect any sign of worry in his voice. "We also need some blessing from above." He looked upward. That did not give me much confidence.

"I hope it will be over soon," I said.

"Just be patient. It will be over in a few more hours," he said.

After struggling with the helm for about two hours, he had to be very tired. I saw the captain struggling with the helm, constantly using his muscle power.

"May I take over the helm? You look tired. You just show me how to do it," I said.

"I am fine. But if you really want to try it out, you can do it," the captain said.

I was elated. He then handed me the helm. I thought it was easy just to hold on to it and correct it to the bearing. But as I began to relax, a giant wave hit the ship. The helm spun to the right with such a force that it knocked my hand off the helm. I considered myself physically strong, but the wave's force surprised me. I struggled to regain the control and put it back to its bearing. But holding it to the same bearing was easier to say than do. I had to concentrate on what I was doing and hold it tightly to stay on course. Otherwise, it could knock off my hand and spin in different directions. At the time, I knew how physically demanding it was to the people behind the helm. The captain saw what happened to me and soon relieved me from the helm. He called the two officers back to relieve him, but he stayed on the bridge—watching.

"We will drive through near the eye of the typhoon soon and the waves will be calmer. And after we pass the eye of typhoon, the waves will be higher again. You may want to stay in your room and make yourself comfortable," he told me.

"I am not tired, and I feel fine. If you allow me to watch the operations, I would like to stay up here," I said.

"You may stay here as you wish, and we will go down for lunch later," he said.

Indeed, the waves and wind soon became less intense. We had entered the eye of Typhoon Bass. At one o'clock in the afternoon, the captain and I went below to rest up a little and met again in the dining hall for lunch. I found that we were the only two persons eating lunch

The Island Heaven

there. The others simply did not have the appetite or were afraid to get sick. The cook on the ship prepared the same amount of food. I ate all the chicken drumsticks I could eat in one meal, but there were so many of them in the large pot. I saw Max was in the dining room taking a nap. I called and woke him up. He was not as alert or playful as he usually acted. When I offered him a whole drumstick, he just looked at me sheepishly for a second and turned his head the other way. I knew for sure now that dogs could get seasick too.

"Max is seasick. He does not even want to eat the chicken drumstick," I told the captain.

"Dogs are just like people. Some of them get seasick and some don't. I had a dog before. She never got seasick," he told me.

"Captain, you must have seen a lot of storms in the past. Is this the biggest one?" I asked.

"Yes, this typhoon is really a big one," he said.

"Are you worried? Do you think we will get through this one alive?" I was worried.

"Of course, I am worried, but it won't do any good. We are trying to do the right thing in a storm and pray to god to protect us from the damn storm." He got a little excited.

"Are you a Buddhism or Christian?" I asked.

"None of them, but I do believe in god," he said.

"May god protect us, whichever god that you believe in," I said. I wished I had gone to church more often in the past. I did not know how to pray correctly when I really needed help. I felt my stomach getting tighter, but I did not feel any nausea.

The Antenna of the Ship

After two hours, the wind and waves came back as fierce as they were before. But this time, the wind was from the opposite direction. The waves kicked up by the typhoon kept pounding on the ship. The ship seemed to be able to keep afloat. I was worried the old ship might break apart under the pressure, or it might be tipped over by a giant wave from the starboard. However, after so many hours, we were still afloat. My confidence to survive this typhoon was greatly increased.

CHAPTER 18

LOST ON THE HIGH SEAS

The night came. I was very tired from the storm and the worry. So, I turned in after supper. Wang was still covering his head in bed. That night, I had a restful sleep. The next morning, I woke up at seven o'clock. The sea was calm, and the sky was clear. I knew the typhoon was over. I put my coat on and rushed to the dining room, where a lot of people were gathered for breakfast, including the captain.

"Good morning, everyone. I assume you all had a scare, but we came out of the typhoon in good shape. You are doing well. Please accept my congratulations!" The captain was in good spirits. He smiled as he greeted us.

"Thank you for your skills to guide the ship in such a storm safely. We thank you very much," Mrs. Goldberg said.

In the next two days, the weather was good, but the officers and sailors were not as happy as I thought they would be. Everyone was tightlipped about what was going on. Only on the fifth day after we had left Typhoon Bass, I detected there was something very wrong. I was worried, so I approached the captain and asked him, "Is there anything wrong with the ship or something?"

"Yes, there is something wrong, but I can't tell you now," the captain said.

When I bumped into Mr. Lee, he had the same concern about the ship, but we couldn't imagine what was the problem.

"What do you think is wrong with the ship?" I asked.

"I don't know, but it must be something went very wrong," Lee said.

"I hope the crew will find a way to fix the problem soon," I said.

On the sixth day, the captain called everyone in the dining hall. "We have some really bad problems on board this ship. Our communications gear is down. The loran and radar are not working as well. Therefore, we don't know our location. In other words, we are lost in the ocean," the captain announced.

Wow! We were lost in the vast ocean! We did not know where we were and did not know what direction we should be going.

"That is very serious! Do you know what is wrong with the equipment?" Lee asked.

"No. We do not know what is wrong with the equipment," the captain answered.

"Do we have anyone on board who can fix this equipment?" Mr. Lee asked.

"We normally maintain our equipment while we are in port. There is no need for us to worry about the equipment," the captain said.

"How about the antennas? They could be damaged in the storm," I asked.

"I have looked at the antennas. They looked just fine," the communications officer said.

"Well, I think they deserve a closer look," I said.

I saw no others offered any solutions. I volunteered my service.

"Captain, the HF radio communication has lost its contact with others. I think I know what is wrong with it. It must be the antenna damaged by the storm," I said.

"Have you checked the connections and the power supplies?" the captain asked the communications officer.

"Yes, I did. But I couldn't find anything wrong with it," the communication officer said.

"It must be caused by the antenna," I said.

"If you insist," the communication officer said, "but we can't possibly fix it now."

"The radar and the loran are also acting funny. They don't work well in the storm anyway," the first mate also reported.

"Now we really don't know where we are, even after the storm. We must fix this equipment," the captain said.

Lost in the ocean in a typhoon? Just what did that mean? How far were we blown by the typhoon away from our normal course? And where we were? The answer was we didn't know.

How come I was so unlucky? I could've borrowed the money to fly to the United States and would've been there months ago. Why did the shipping company let the ship sail while knowing there was a typhoon coming to it path? Maybe they did not even know about the pending typhoon. And how about my wife and my parents? They must be worried sick to learn about the typhoon in the ocean between Taiwan and Japan! That was the first time since we left Taiwan, I felt very sick in my heart.

CHAPTER 19

HANDY MAN ON BOARD

Twenty-four hours after Typhoon Bass hit the ship, the wind started to subside. The sky became clearer and the waves were still high but were no longer threatening. The remaining days, the weather was so good that we were all very relaxed until the captain gave the bad news. He held the news from the passengers to not scare us. But now he had to let us know about the truth.

"Because of the typhoon, we have lost the ship's exact bearing. The antennas of the loran, radar, and the radio transmitter were all severely damaged. We are not able to contact other ships or the land stations. Without such equipment functioning, we could lose days just to figure out how to get to where we want to go," the captain announced. There was the silence. I was sure that I could fix it, but I was afraid of being too forward. But since there was no other person who wanted to help, I volunteered my services.

"Captain, do you have electronic technicians on board the ship?" I asked.

"Unfortunately, no. But we have electricians on board. You are familiar with the antennas?" he asked.

"I am familiar with the equipment and the antennas. If you give me two electricians to assist me, I will repair them for you," I said with confidence.

"You really can fix them for us?" the captain looked at me and said.

"Yes. I am sure I can fix them, because that was my specialty. I have worked on the radio transmitters for many years," I said.

"You are a godsend! I will provide you with anything we have to fix the equipment," said the captain.

"I will start right away. When your guys are ready," I told the captain.

The captain was much relieved because there was no one in the ranks of officers or crew members who had experience with radio equipment or antennas.

It was in the midmorning. The weather was as good as it could be. I took two sailors with me. We climbed up to the top of the ship's superstructure, where the antennas were installed. It was not easy to get up there while the ship was moving. The wind was not as strong as during the storm, but it was still fierce enough to blow one into the water if not holding on to a fixture of the ship. And it was very cold.

When we reached the top of the superstructure, we found the tangle of wires, masts, and debris. A piece of heavy object had smashed around where the antennas were anchored. We found the tangled wire of the RF antenna. I untangled it and fixed it onto the terminals. We took the deformed VHF antennas down to the deck. A machinist straightened out the mast with whatever tools he had available on board the ship. I removed some short circuits that were caused by dents and burns. We then put the antennas back on top of the ship. The loran first worked, and then the radio transmitter was confirmed working when we received the acknowledgment from another ship. Finally, we fixed the radar's wave guides that were bent out of shape. The communications officer was beaming, and the captain was elated.

This repair work took us one solid day to complete. And we were very tired. The captain and the officers were very happy.

"Tien-Ren, you sure have saved my day. You know, without the equipment, we could get lost in the ocean. Thank you very much, my friend," the captain said while he patted my back.

"You are most welcome, Captain. It is my life too. I don't want to get lost in the ocean either," I joked.

As a gesture to thank me for repairing the antennas and testing the radio transmitter/receiver, the captain sent a telegraph to my parents just to tell them we had survived the typhoon. When he told me about that afterward, I could imagine how frightened my mom, dad, and wife would be when the telegraph arrived at my home. In Taiwan in those days, only death and the most urgent matters were sent by telegraph—no news was good news. A telegraph came from the shipping company while we were hit by a Typhoon. That must be bad news! I appreciated the captain's goodwill, but I wished he had not done it. I prayed Mom and Dad wouldn't be overly frightened by the telegraph when it was handed to them. How about my wife? How would she react to the telegraph before seeing the content? I was really feeling sick when I thought about it. But I just thanked the captain for his goodwill.

After the officers determined the ship's location with the loran, we were told that the ship was very close to Japan and we could reach there within four days. The original plan was going straight to the west coast of the United States. Upon confirming the order from the shipping company, the captain again called a meeting of officers and passengers.

"We have a change of plans. We are steering toward Tokyo and Yokohama to pick up some cargo before heading for the United States," the captain said. "Any problems with you passengers?"

No one had any objection.

"We will make a stop in Tokyo for about three days and Yokohama for two days," the captain continued.

"Can we go on shore in Japan?" Wang asked.

"Not only you can go on shore, I will give you a tour you will never forget!" the captain told us.

"That's great! I would like to visit the electronics street in Tokyo," I said. "Can you take us there just for a short stop?" I was afraid the other students might make objections.

The Island Heaven

"I want to go there as well. I need a short-wave radio," Mr. Lee said.

"Fine, we will stop by the electronics street and have lunch there," the captain promised.

The passengers were very happy that we had a chance to see both Tokyo and Yokohama. As we steamed closer to the island country, in the harbor, I could smell an odor I had experienced previously in an abalone market. The ship anchored in the harbor of Yokohama, about half of a mile from the shore, and for two days we did not go to shore. There were droves of vendors climbing aboard to sell apples, dress shirts, and other small items. Some sailors bought apples and clothing items.

"The items you buy from these vendors are much more expensive than you buy in the United States," a sailor told me.

I had never eaten any apples before in my life. I was attracted by their looks and smell, but they were very costly. I told myself that I needed to conserve my limited supply of money. I bought only two apples for about $1.10. But the apple made me so sick for the rest of the day. I was vomiting and having stomach pains all that day but recovered overnight. I knew it was caused by not washing the apple thoroughly.

Two days later in the morning, the ship left for Tokyo.

Throughout the war with Japan during the World War II, and in peacetime, I had never seen a Japanese in person. My impression of the Japanese people was based on the news reports and stories told to me during the war. In my mind, they were short, ugly, greedy, cruel, and aggressive. I hated the Japanese people, for they were our enemies that caused so much death and destruction in China. I had not forgotten my grandma, grandpa, sister, and brother were all dead as a result of the Japanese invasion. Just in my birthplace—Nanjing—they had slaughtered over 300,000 innocent civilians in a matter of six weeks. Now I was going to face those people face-to-face in a close encounter!

In Yokohama, the boat vendors were the first few Japanese I had seen with my own eyes. They looked very much like the Chinese street vendors begging sailors to buy, haggling on prices over their meager merchandise, exactly as I had seen in the back streets of Taipei. I had hated the Japanese for most of my life. Now that I had closer contact, I saw that they were indeed short. Some were ugly, but there were some good-looking ones. They were humble and polite, just trying to make a few dollars for a living. I began to wonder. Did I place my anger toward the right direction? Might it be just the leader or the leaders of the people that drove them to commit those unspeakable crimes? Was the cruelty committed in World War II the normal behavior of the common Japanese people? I still could not forget what the Japanese had done to the Chinese during the war. I was quite confused at that moment in time.

After the ship anchored in Tokyo Harbor, Captain Ouyang helped us to get a temporary permit to visit Tokyo. In order to cheer up his officers and the passengers, the captain and the four officers took the three of us ashore. Mrs. Goldberg did not feel well enough to take the tour. We left the ship at about three o'clock in the afternoon. Our first stop was to Ginza, a district in Tokyo famous for its stripteases.

"I am going to take you to the strip dance theater. Any objections?"

The captain had to be joking.

"I don't mind. I have never seen anything like that," Wang said.

"I don't mind seeing it either," I said. "It was something I had never heard of or seen in Taiwan."

"I like to see that. It is a must when you are in Tokyo," Lee said, half jokingly.

With high curiosity and anticipation, we arrived at Ginza by subway train in early evening. The captain treated us with the sushi and sashimi dinner. These were considered luxury items and were very expensive in Taiwan. Those were not the kind of food that a college instructor could afford to have. I really did not like the taste of the raw seafood and ordered fried fish instead. After dinner, the captain led us to a theater across street. The tickets were not cheap, but the captain paid them all.

The theater was small but well lit. The stage was just like a regular stage with an artificial stage background. It started with some comedians then the real show started. A troupe of young topless women came from behind the stage and danced in all sorts of formations. It was very interesting to all the students with eyes popping out of their sockets. The show lasted only about forty minutes.

We had a really good time that evening. I found the Japanese people were very polite and cordial toward visitors. One thing we were not quite used to be the constant bowing from the store clerks and the waitresses. We simply did not know what to do when they bowed to us.

"Just smile and do not pay much attention to them," the captain said to us.

When we went back to the ship, it was almost midnight.

The next day at about ten o'clock, the captain again took us to the shore of Tokyo by a small boat. He then took us by train to the shopping district of Tokyo and to visit the famous electronics street, where hundreds of electronics shops were located. We walked through camera shops, radio shops, and some clothing stores. It was very interesting seeing all these gadgets and fancy electronics products. But not much money changed hand during the day when we were there. None of the three students had any money to buy things.

At the last moment, I could not resist the urge to buy a camera. I spent forty-two dollars to buy a Yashica SLR camera, which was about half of the money I had then. My justification was the need to record the rest of the trip on the ship and my one to two years living in the States. The third day we took a long ride in the Tokyo subway and elevated train throughout the city. My observation was that the middle-aged and older Japanese were very short. Most of them were about five feet, three or less. The younger generations were much taller. They averaged five, seven or taller. On the trains, I was taller than the great majority with my five seven inches height, which was about the average height for my generation in Taiwan. The captain paid the bills for the train fares and all meals. We thanked him for his generosity and thoughtfulness. He told us the shipping company authorized him to spend the money to treat us because of the extra time it took for the trip and our suffering from the typhoon. I thought that was very nice of the shipping company.

CHAPTER 20

ARRIVING IN MY DREAMLAND

The three-day stay in Tokyo went quickly. On the fourth day early in the morning, the ship left Tokyo Bay and continued its journey to the United States of America. It was a gloomy day with light rain when the ship left Tokyo Harbor. The air quality in Tokyo was very poor indeed. Just about all the passengers started coughing on the second day in Tokyo. We were happy to be on the high seas again just to be able to breathe the clean air. We felt our lungs were refreshed after the ship was thirty minutes out to the open sea. Our destination was Longview City in Washington State. The weather for the rest of the way was very good. The ship pushed forward in the calm water uneventfully.

"Tien-Ren, your hair is so long that it makes you looked like a bandit. Why don't you let me cut your hair for you?" the captain said to me.

I looked at myself from the reflection of the window; my long hair did make me look very sloppy. So, I reluctantly agreed because I did not think a ship's captain could be a good barber. He turned out to be much better than I thought.

"I have been cutting hair for my three sons for years. I am experienced, you see! Just look at the mirror," he told me.

"Why don't you cut the hair for the other two fellows? They also look awful," I said.

"I do this for you because you have done a big favor to us by fixing the ship's antennas. I really don't have the time or the interest to cut their hair," he said.

The captain and two officers of the ship also gave me a big bag of green tea and a small pack of dried beef sticks as parting gifts.

"Thank you for giving me so many gifts, but I have nothing to give you," I said to the captain and the first mate.

"You don't have to give us anything. What you have done for us is more than we could give you. We need to thank you. Believe me," said the first mate, Mr. Liu.

In the early morning of October 16, 1961, I saw for the first time the United States' mainland just a short distance away. A surge of feelings and thoughts rushed through my mind. First, it was such a beautiful country. *What kind of people am I going to live among? Am I going to be accepted by teachers and other students? What are the right things to do, and what are the right ways to express myself?* I was very concerned about my language deficiency. I had special difficulty listening to and understanding the stream of words in a sentence. *Will they be upset if I do not understand their words and sentences?*

I still have the images of Americans' fist punches from the movies. I really thought the Americans were hot-tempered people and were very intolerant. I also thought about my wife, my son, and my parents and how they had been since I left Taiwan. Now that I was totally alone to face the new world, I was a bit worrisome about my lack of understanding of this new land. But I was more excited about entering this strongest, richest, and technologically most advanced country in the world. I wanted to learn as much as I could while I had the opportunity before I returned to Taiwan.

As the ship moved closer to the land, I could clearly see the landscape, the residential houses, the huge office structures, and the green-treed mountains. Unlike in Japan where thick, dark-gray smog covered the cities, the air was clear. I took several deep breaths to sample the fresh air. I instantly felt quite good about where I was going and anxious to see what else was in this new land for me to discover.

Longview was a city upriver from the bay. The ship was guided by a pilot who came on board as the ship was at the entry point of the river, to navigate the waterway upstream. Along the river, I saw beautiful farmhouses and large farmland. The air was quite cold inland on this October morning. It took about one hour to reach the city dock. The ship was tied down on the pier along with many other ocean liners. My impression was the orderly and neatness of the usually crowded and badly polluted harbor, as I had seen before this.

The captain told us that the immigration officers and the customs agents would be boarding the ship at eight o'clock. After that, if we had some time, we could go ashore for breakfast in a restaurant. At eight o'clock sharp, four uniformed officers came on board the ship. We put our papers in order and presented our luggage for inspection. At eight twenty, two officers came to my cabin. I assumed one was immigration officer and the other one was the customs officer. They looked over my papers, asked no questions, but just gave me a card called I-94.

"Whatever you do, be sure not to lose this card," one of the officers told me. Then they stamped my passport and gave it back to me. I was formally admitted into the United States. It was the dream come true since I'd decided to come and study in the United States.

"Are you carrying any vegetable or meat products with you?" another officer asked me.

"No," I said confidently. I had forgotten the beef strips the captain had given me. At about eight thirty-five, I was successfully processed by the custom and immigration services. They then continued to check my roommate while the others were still waiting to be processed.

I went to the shore alone to test myself in this totally strange land. Other passengers stayed on the ship, waiting for their turn. It was about eight forty-five in the morning. It struck me how clean the streets were and how all the buildings were so well maintained. They looked as neat as I had ever seen anywhere. The streets were

The Island Heaven

not crowded with people. I saw just one or two people walking on the street. There were no street vendors trying to push their goods. As a matter of fact, I felt the street was too quiet and was wondering whether I could walk around freely.

I walked into a small restaurant and sat by a tiny table. There were several customers eating food and drinking coffee nearby. A young waitress came to my table and gave me a menu. I looked over the pages of the menu; I did not understand the meaning of most words. I figured that I wanted to eat a good breakfast, so I pointed to a line with a price equal to a good dinner in Taipei, which was NT$4 or equivalent to ten US cents.

"That all, sir?" The waitress was surprised by my order. I nodded my head. I was wondering what I had ordered. In a couple of minutes, the girl brought out a small dish of Jell-O. When I saw that, I knew what a Jell-O was. I was suddenly not hungry anymore. I put a dime on the table, rushed out of the restaurant, and went back to the ship.

By then, the officials had cleared all the passengers. We were ready to leave the ship. The captain came to us to say good-bye. He gave me his home address in Taipei and wished to keep in touch. I said good-bye to the officers and a few sailors as well as the three other passengers. I said good-bye to Mr. Wang and Mr. Lee in Chinese. Mr. Lee's eyes welled with tears. He quickly turned to the other direction and walked off. Mr. Wang simply said good-bye and walked away. Mrs. Goldberg hired a taxi and drove off. We were going our separate ways and never saw one another again.

Longview, Washington, was the city I first set my feet down on in the United States. Full of curiosity and not knowing what to expect, I saw a very clean city with wide streets and neat buildings. There were very few people on the street in the midmorning. Many cars were parked on the curbs of streets and a few of them were moving orderly on the street. Not a single policeman was in sight. I was not used to such quietness on a major street of a city. The few people on the street were going to places in a hurried pace. No one was sitting around the street corner or chatting on the street. The much-anticipated street fights were nowhere to be seen. It was a port city, but I did not smell any fish odor. As a matter of fact, I felt the air in Longview fresh and pure, free of any detectable pollutant. That very day, the sky was in deep blue and very clear. The few people I encountered were very nice, polite, and friendly. The fear in me of being punched on the nose by strangers began to melt away. A surge of relief, peace, and joyful feelings filled my heart.

I liked this land the first day I arrived here. It was not at all as I had perceived in my mind, based on overseas media and movie stars. That was the first time I had real contact with white people. My first impression of white people was that their eye colors were not all blue, as I thought, and the hair colors also had a wide range of variations. Some people had light blue/gray eyes that looked to me as if they had no eyeballs. I was so used to seeing black or dark-brown eyes all my life.

I took a bus to Portland, Oregon, which was a hub of Greyhound Bus. I went to the Greyhound bus station to buy a ticket to Menomonie, Wisconsin. The ticket agent turned the pages on that big, thick book and said to me, "It is not in the book and I have never heard of the place before." He then asked me, "Are you sure it's Menomonie, Wisconsin, and not Menomonee, Michigan? I have never heard of the place in my eight years working here."

I had a sinking feeling. If the Greyhound agent did not know how to find a route going to my school, I would be stuck here for good. I knew I was correct about the address, since I had correspondence with the school. In order to prove my point, I pulled out and showed him the letter from Dr. Wigen. He then waved the letter and asked his associate, a young man who sat next to him, "Do you know where this place is?"

"Oh! Just go to Eau Clair and transfer to Menomonie. It is about thirty miles away from Eau Clair," the young man said.

The agent gave me two tickets and said, "You owe me $39.65 for the entire trip. When you get to Eau Clair, check with the agents there. They will tell you which bus to take to get you to Menomonie."

After I paid the tickets, the agent told me the estimated time of arrival at Menomonie. I found a coin-operated phone booth, called

The Island Heaven

the graduate program's office at Stout, and told the secretary about my arrival.

"This is Catherine Olson, the dean of graduate programs office. May I help you?" the voice at the other end said.

"This is Richard Cheng from Taiwan. I am on my way to Menomonie from Portland, Oregon. I should be in school two days from now," I said in broken English.

"What time are you going to be in Menomonie?" she asked me slowly.

"The bus will be arriving at about six thirty in the afternoon on the eighteenth," I told her, again in broken English. But she seemed to understand what I said. My purpose was just to notify the school that I was in the country and was a few days late to register for classes.

"Okay. We'll see you in a day or so. Bye!" She hung up the phone. The operator told me to put in another fifty cents.

At that point, at least I knew I had found the city I wanted to go to. I felt much more comfortable now with my first morning in this new country. People here seemed not that much different from my homeland, except they all looked different and talked so fast. I had a really hard time listening and translating at the same time. The bus was to leave in just ten minutes. I grabbed my suitcase and the box of books and presented the ticket to the driver. There was just one uniformed person running this huge bus. He was the driver, ticket person, and the luggage man. He punched a hole on my ticket, picked up my two pieces of luggage, and placed them under the lower compartment of the bus. I was very impressed with the efficiency and the good attitude of the bus driver. I thought, *no wonder this country is so rich and powerful. This bus driver is doing a job that would take three people to do in some other countries.*

As I sat down in the numbered seat, while the bus was waiting for others to board, I closed my eyes just to gather my thoughts. I thought, *Finally, I am in the dreamland I had been longing for.* But I was 10,000 miles away from my home, my roots, and my loved ones. Suddenly a feeling of loneliness set in. There was no one I could talk to and no one here would care about me whatsoever. All I had was just hope and thousands of unanswered questions.

Printed in the USA
CPSIA information can be obtained
at www.ICGtesting.com
LVHW090105110224
771408LV00003B/388